Praise for *UNLOCK*

An engaging read, *UNLOCK* presents leaders with an important challenge: to access the untapped potential within people, particularly those that appear disengaged. Ishan skilfully weaves personal anecdotes, relatable analogies, and global case studies into his storytelling, creating a narrative that will connect with leaders seeking inspiration for respectful, practical, tangible change, both for their people and their organisations.

– **Rebecca Michalik, President, Association for Manufacturing Excellence (AME) Australia**

For all supply chain leaders who want to *UNLOCK* the secret to creating an engaged workplace and foster that community culture, this book is a must read. *UNLOCK* champions the belief that every employee holds the key to a collective success. It outlines a transformative journey for businesses, igniting teams through a culture of improvement and inclusivity. Ishan's storytelling brings the simple, yet effective, framework to life, making it an easy read. I highly recommend this book as a 'go to' almanac to unlocking productivity and engagement.

– **Sue Tomic, Chairperson, Supply Chain and Logistics Association of Australia (SCLAA)**

A compelling guide for leaders and organisations aiming to transform their workplace culture and enhance employee engagement. The holy grail of every business! Ishan's narrative is rich with data, anecdotes, personal experience and global case studies providing a multifaceted view of the issue at hand. The strength of the book lies in his framework, designed to incrementally engage disengaged employees through strategic inclusion in key projects and initiatives. This will be a valuable resource for leaders seeking to revitalise their workforce and harness the full potential of their teams.

– **Les Wingham, Chief Operating Officer,**
Industry Partners Australia

Engagement – if ever there was a word for our time, then this is it. It embodies the connectivity consumers crave; it's the crux of sales success; it drives business performance – and yet we are facing a disengagement crisis. Ishan Galapathy's latest book, *UNLOCK*, is timely and useful to anyone running a business today. It unpacks the meaning of true engagement and gives practical guidance on how to unlock the latent capacity of the disengaged employees to propel your business forward.

– **Lindy Hughson, Managing Editor & Publisher,**
PKN Packaging News (Yaffa Media)

Amidst global upheavals, engaged teams prove vital for organisational resilience and success. In today's competitive landscape, post-pandemic challenges highlight the necessity of integrating sustainability strategies and front-line worker engagement. While technology offers advancements, unlocking the potential of supply chain teams remains paramount for true productivity. *UNLOCK*'s approach harnesses talent and experience, empowering businesses to lead and adapt amidst change. Ishan's insights hit the mark once more!

– **Craig Funnell, retired Chief Supply Officer, Arnott's Group, 40-year veteran of global supply chains across multiple regions**

UNLOCK is a great read in the realm of organisational excellence. Ishan's blend of storytelling and practical advice makes it a compelling read for leaders at all levels. Whether you're leading a small team or a multinational corporation, *UNLOCK* offers invaluable insights into driving meaningful change and maximising productivity.

– **Paul Serra, Group CEO, SunRice**

In his true style, Ishan has found a way to make the concepts of lean and organisational excellence come to life by giving his ingenious touches to how we can apply them to accelerate change adoption and business transformation. *UNLOCK* is relatable to all leaders out there who want to mobilise their workforce to excel. This is certainly a book that you will want to keep handy as you navigate the morphing challenges in this post-pandemic world. The experiential anecdotes are a great asset to share with your teams as you influence them to deliver unbelievable outcomes!

> **– Maha Rajagopalan, Program Management Office (Business Transformation), ResMed**

UNLOCK is a game-changer and addresses the vital behavioural and cultural elements of a meaningful operational excellence journey. Real life examples across multiple industries provide an entertaining read with outstanding tools and tactics that can directly translate into results.

> **– Mike Allen, VP North America Manufacturing, Haleon**

If you believe in the power of engaged people to deliver extraordinary results but, like many workplaces, are challenged to unlock this power, Ishan's latest work is for you. *UNLOCK* has provided a toolkit on how to engage and unlock the power of people explained using practical real-life examples.

    – Tim Morgan, Chief Supply Officer, Arnott's Group

In *UNLOCK*, Ishan delivers a masterclass in unlocking the potential of those who appear disconnected or uninterested. His three-step *UNLOCK* flywheel framework provides a roadmap for fostering genuine engagement and igniting passion in every interaction. This book is a must read for anyone seeking to cultivate meaningful connections and drive positive change.

    – Holly Smith, Head of Talent and Organisational Development, GWA Group

In *UNLOCK*, Ishan's style of storytelling really connects the reader to the key concepts targeted at engaging a team. This is a relevant and important subject in finding the path forward in achieving high performance with a great team culture.

    – Kari Banick, Chief Operating Officer, Blackwoods

UNLOCK is easily digestible and speaks to readers in very clear and straightforward terms using compelling anecdotes. This book has inspired me with great ideas to shift the dial in some of my key programs of work. I have read many operational excellence and lean books that are more academic in style and misaligned with the current industry requirements. *UNLOCK* bridges this yawning gap. It is a must read that will help you deliver outstanding results with a strong focus on employee engagement.

– Manu Liyanarachchi, National Operational Excellence Manager, Coca Cola Europacific Partners (CCEP)

UNLOCK is a game-changer for anyone looking to break through barriers in communication and connection. With insightful strategies and practical advice, this book empowers readers to bridge the gap between disengagement and active participation, fostering genuine engagement and collaboration. A must-read for leaders, educators and anyone seeking to unlock the full potential of those around them.

– Abdul Jaafar, Executive General Manager Supply Chain, Bapcor Limited

The engaging style of *UNLOCK* highlights that everyone has a contribution to give that will draw success out for all. It provides a path to ignite its people and build a high-performing team by the infectiousness of improvement and success. A great read. Highly recommend it.

– **Chris Poole, Senior Area Business Manager Operations, UGL Unipart**

UNLOCK masterfully addresses the perennial challenge of fostering genuine employee engagement. Through compelling storytelling and practical frameworks, Galapathy not only diagnoses the widespread issue of workplace disengagement, but also prescribes a practical methodology to invigorate the 'quiet quitters'. This book is a beacon for leaders striving for operational excellence and a motivated workforce. Galapathy's insights are both profound and actionable, offering a clear path to unlocking the potential of every team member. *UNLOCK* is an essential read for anyone committed to elevating their organisational culture and achieving unparalleled results.

– **Amit Ranga, Managing Director, Majans Pty Ltd**

Many organisations have the best intentions to improve employee engagement but struggle to take the next steps beyond the annual survey while focusing too much time on the actively disengaged. *UNLOCK* outlines practical and inarguable steps to follow from making that important and meaningful start right through to creating a sustainable flywheel of momentum.

– Dean Patton, Head of Operations and Continuous Improvement for various Australian and Global organisations

UNLOCK offers a refreshing perspective on engaging seemingly disengaged individuals by taking them on a journey. It effectively addresses the key question of how you shift the dial in employee engagement. *UNLOCK* provides valuable insights into building momentum, fostering trust and engaging stakeholders to build a positive culture and drive productivity. *UNLOCK* is a practical read for individuals and organisations to build strong foundations in improving employee engagement.

– Hemandra Maharaj, Primary Freight Manager, Metcash Trading Ltd.

UNLOCK offers readers a comprehensive deployment framework and methodology for engaging people in organisational change. What sets this book apart is its ability to simplify complex concepts into easily understandable steps, often aided by simple relatable examples drawn from the author's personal experiences. *UNLOCK* serves as a valuable resource for organisations seeking to navigate the intricacies of change management, propelling them towards excellence in operations across various industries. It's a true gem that demystifies the engagement process and paves the way for achieving world-class standards. Highly recommend *UNLOCK* for anyone looking on embarking on a transformational journey.

– **Jay Dixit, Head of Supply Chain,**
De'Longhi Australia PTY LTD

It is not often I read a book that is both simple and profound at the same time: rooted in solid principles and theories, yet absolutely practical as well. If you are a leader who is serious about driving excellence, *UNLOCK* is certainly a must read!

– **Vidusha Nathavitharana, Founding**
Director, Luminary Learning Solutions

UNLOCK presents a human-centred approach as a precursor to change and improvements. It reminds us that unlocking requires intention and that 'progress is (indeed) infectious and exciting'. *UNLOCK* helps the reader to target and refocus on people using Ishan's wealth of experience helping organisations become more efficient, more productive and certainly more engaged. The candid and straightforward style invites readers on a clear journey toward positive transformation. *UNLOCK* offers a gift of wisdom to changemakers, business leaders and enthusiasts, urging them to prioritise people as they drive sustainable improvements within their teams and organisations.

– Yelitza Guerra, Global Head of Operations, Rhino-Rack

Having led many operational excellence programs globally for major multinational companies, I know the effort required to get such programs off the ground and embedded into the organisational culture. Ishan's latest book, *UNLOCK*, offers a powerful framework that cuts out the guess work and provides a simple recipe to make a real difference. A must read for any leader who's been waiting for an effective roadmap to unlock excellence in organisations.

– Joe Russo, Chief Supply Chain Officer, Accolade Wines

UNLOCK

Also by Ishan Galapathy

*Hidden Growth Opportunities:
10 Paradigms Why World-Class
Companies Are More Efficient*

Understand why the best-of-the best global manufacturing companies always stay a step ahead, irrespective of external forces and input costs.

*ADVANCE:
12 Essential Elements to Supercharge
Productivity and Profitability*

Your simple, paint-by-numbers operational excellence guide complete with step-by-step instructions, frameworks and templates to fast track your journey to excellence.

UNLOCK

Engage the
Seemingly Disengaged

ISHAN GALAPATHY

Copyright © Ishan Galapathy

All models copyright © Ishan Galapathy

First published in 2024 by Bison Press

Model design by Celeste Davidson
celestedavidsonfreelance@gmail.com

Typeset in Australia by BookPOD

All rights reserved. No part of this publication may be reproduced by any means without the prior written consent of the publisher.

This book uses stories to enforce the meaning behind its relevant chapter. Permission to use these stories has been provided.

Every effort has been made to trace (and seek permission for use of) the original source of material used within this book. Where the attempt has been unsuccessful, the publisher would be pleased to hear from the author/publisher to rectify any omission.

ISBN: 978-0-6451120-1-6 eISBN: 978-0-6451120-2-3

A catalogue record for this book is available from the National Library of Australia

Contents

Introduction: Why Is it Hard to Soar Like an Eagle? 1
We've Missed the Obvious 11
The UNLOCK Method and Framework.................. 14
The UNLOCK Philosophy.. 18
The UNLOCK Framework.. 20

STEP 1
Build Momentum 23
Chapter 1: Value Your Values 32
Chapter 2: Believe in Them.. 46
Chapter 3: What's Your Side Hustle? 66

STEP 2
Gain Traction 77
Chapter 4: It's Not Me; it's You! 88
Chapter 5: Give it a Go 100
Chapter 6: SMART Factories and DUMB Operators 112
Chapter 7: Start with Who 126
Chapter 8: Flaws and Fortunes 138
Chapter 9: Adapting to Triumph 148

STEP 3
EXPAND FOLLOWERS 163

Chapter 10: Name it 172

Chapter 11: Leverage Their Ego 190

Chapter 12: A Rising Tide Lifts All Boats 206

Conclusion 221

UNLOCK Leadership Assessment 229

Actions to UNLOCK Your Team/Organisation 231

About the Author 241

Acknowledgements 243

References 247

Dedication

I would like to dedicate this book to my very first manager, Paul Martin, who hired me to work over the summer holidays when I was a university student. It was 1997 and Sydney, Australia, was gearing up to host the Sydney 2000 Olympics, which meant a lot of construction and development.

Paul was the operations manager of a large aluminium windows and doors manufacturer. Given the boom in construction, the demand from this factory was increasing rapidly. It was an old factory with multiple buildings, which meant poor workflow. With nearly 150 people working in different work centres, my task was simple – assist the team to improve productivity in the factory. This is how I got started in continuous improvement.

Paul gave me a crash course in concepts such as TQM (total quality management), time-and-motion analysis, and he gave me one very important tip – spend time in the factory, work with the operators to understand things that go wrong. He had a lot of time for me and helped me to progress in my career.

Trying to understand operator frustrations and getting them involved to resolve those issues is how I still operate. It is also the very essence of this book.

Unfortunately, Paul passed away in 2019 in his mid-50s, leaving behind his beautiful wife Angela and two adult children. I'm grateful for the opportunities, lessons and guidance Paul provided, without which I would not have ended up doing what I do. He was a wonderful person.

Rest in peace Paul.

Preface

In 2018, I was working with a client who manufactures and distributes frozen bakery products. I came across the following fable on the wall next to the production manager's desk.

This is a story about four people named Everybody, Somebody, Anybody and Nobody.

There was an important job to be done and Everybody was sure that Somebody would do it.

Anybody could have done it, but Nobody did it.

Somebody got angry because it was Everybody's job.

Everybody thought that Anybody could do it, but Nobody realised that Everybody wouldn't do it.

In the end Everybody blamed Somebody when Nobody did what Anybody could do.

– author unknown

It stuck in my head and since then I have often reflected on the essence of this fable – employees who don't care about their work and workplace.

On a separate but related point, I take an interest in keeping a pulse check on two global trends – the Gallup employee engagement results and Gartner's global top 25 supply chain announcements. Both of these are released annually.

When analysing the overall Gallup engagement results, I can see that the essence of the fable is validated undisputedly through global data. I do a deep dive of this in the introduction section, but in a nutshell, 50–60% of employees are not engaged (are disengaged) and it is costing businesses around US$8.8 trillion globally, or 9% of the global GDP. That's a lot!

Looking at the top performers on Gartner's top 25 list, it's clear that there's a reason why most of those well-known companies end up at the top. They have 'operational excellence' frameworks and methodologies truly embedded to deliver outstanding results year after year. Unsurprisingly, the employee engagement numbers of those companies are better than the average.

My book, *ADVANCE: 12 Essential Elements to Supercharge Productivity and Profitability,* provides a simplified, paint-by-numbers, operational excellence framework that you could deploy to deliver great results, year on year. This book, *UNLOCK: Engage the Seemingly Disengaged*, addresses the other key issue: employee engagement. The UNLOCK concept outlines how I work with my clients, deploying the ADVANCE framework and improving their employee engagement numbers as an outcome.

So, with *ADVANCE* providing you with the nuts and bolts of an operational excellence framework and *UNLOCK* with the methodology for its deployment, you've got both the *what* and the *how*. Therefore, there's no reason why you can't deliver exceptional results like those in Gartner's top list and have an engagement culture in the upper quartile as defined by Gallup.

Something to bear in mind: with over 25 years' experience in supply chain – manufacturing to be precise – my views and methodologies are biased towards this sector. However, the concepts in this book are readily transferable to any sector that operates with teams working with teams (i.e., multiple team levels in the organisation).

If you're a senior leader deploying any operational excellence framework, not just ADVANCE, or embarking on any major change initiative, then flick through this book to get some ideas on how to get quick traction, amplified results and a positive culture. This is the 'journey' I refer to throughout this book.

The other words I use regularly are 'projects' and 'initiatives'. These are the broken-down, bite-sized activities to be deployed in small cross-functional teams as part of your master plan or annual strategic plan. They are the steps of your journey. They could be either problems that are haemorrhaging money from your profit and loss (P&L) statement that need to be solved, or strategic opportunities that could propel your business forward. I explain these in detail in *ADVANCE*, but the explanation here should provide you with a sufficient conceptual overview to bring the *UNLOCK* ideas alive.

Each chapter is a specific idea along with a personal experience and a global case study. Collectively, they provide a simplified yet potent framework for you to move that dial of employee engagement while focusing on increasing productivity.

I wish you all the best.

Ishan Galapathy

Excellence is a journey to be travelled, not completed.

INTRODUCTION

Why Is it Hard to Soar Like an Eagle?

Jim is not your average factory leader – he runs it like it's his own business. I know this sentiment gets thrown around in corporate offices a lot, but in this case, Jim is actually an employee who also runs a separate business of his own as well. There is no conflict of interest, and his employer knows this. So, Jim has a unique set of skills to lead a site and truly run it like his own business.

Jim has been around for a while and is a no-nonsense guy. Everyone knows when he's in the office. He gives 100% all the time, doesn't have a slow gear, challenges anyone for what he believes to be true and right, and expects the same from everyone in his factory – nothing wrong with that. Jim has a great track record in turning businesses around, and when I met him, he had only been with this business for about 18 months. In that time, he'd given the tree a good shake and the positive results were getting noticed in the monthly performance reports (P&L) and at the head office.

He had so many good ideas. 'I was just warming up', he told me once during our early meetings. However, his team didn't have enough bandwidth to execute *all* the ideas, projects, initiatives, improvements and equipment upgrades while running the day-to-day business as well. This was Jim's frustration. He wanted to do so much in a short time, but his team couldn't keep up. 'How do I soar like an eagle, Ishan?' was a question he regularly asked over coffee in his office.

The biggest issue was that he had an extremely lean team and their capability to lead change initiatives was low. For context, I consider change initiatives to be anything from productivity improvement initiatives to new equipment installations, new product introductions to strategy deployment, because all these activities require buy-in from other employees to change the way things are done in the workplace.

Over the next 15 months, we worked together to involve more people in carrying the weight of the team, not just the handful Jim had been relying on so far. We initially started the journey with the few good soldiers he had. It was a journey to excellence, a systematic approach to getting more done with what you have – both equipment and employees.

After the first quarter, the results were already noticeable. By the 15-month mark, the site had a different vibe, a better level of energy and a new way of operating.

The bottom line? The engagement and the culture improved in leaps and bounds, which pleasantly surprised the business.

The other factories in the network wanted to grab some of this talent from Jim's site. They also wanted some of this magic, the secret sauce, the recipe to turn around their site as well. Perhaps you feel like grabbing some of these individuals to turn around your team. The truth is that you don't have to.

> I wonder whether you've overlooked the biggest asset you have.

Many businesses have tried to turn around teams and deliver exceptional results like we did at Jim's site with mixed results. Perhaps you've tried too and feel that it is not that easy. I wonder whether you've overlooked the biggest asset you have, which doesn't appear on your balance sheet – your employees who are quiet and don't want to get involved much.

The secret to this approach is unlocking the latent capacity from these seemingly disengaged employees. That's it. Now, I know what you're thinking. Where are these so-called 'seemingly disengaged employees' and how do you identify them if they are the biggest non-financial asset of the business?

Gallup, a global company based in the US specialising in all things relating to people and employee engagement, has been measuring the engagement levels of employees since the year 2000. In all their publications, they categorise the engagement levels of employees into the following three types.

1. **Engaged**: These employees are the committed, loyal, diligent, caring, enthusiastic high performers who've always got your back. You know who these are in your organisation as there are not that many. This accounted for 23% globally in Gallup's 2022 measurements.

2. **Actively disengaged**: These employees, unfortunately, don't see anything being right in the world. They are unhappy, ill-mouthing, sabotaging, manipulating, blaming individuals who take up a lot of your time, focus and energy. You know who these people are. This group represented 18% in 2022 globally.

3. **Not engaged (disengaged)**: This is the type of individual who falls into the middle: they are not engaged nor actively disengaged. Gallup refers to this category as 'not engaged', and I call it disengaged. These employees turn up in body only, without their creative, brilliant, enthusiastic

and energetic mindset. This is the group that I'm interested in.

How do you find them? Easy. You know who falls into the other two categories: engaged and actively disengaged. The rest fall into this category. 'Quiet quitters' is a term that's been gaining some popularity recently and it quite aptly describes this group. Gallup listed this group as 59% in 2022, globally.

Figure 1 shows the global trend for the above three types, based on Gallup data.

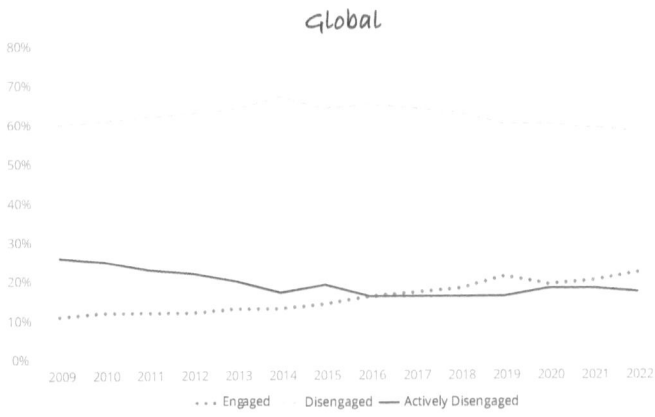

Figure 1: Gallup data demonstrating the year-on-year trend for engaged, actively disengaged and disengaged segments of the workforce.

So, what's wrong with this picture? Yes, the engagement needle is trending up slowly. I bet you'd agree with me that it has been nothing short of hard work even to get to this point, right? So, why haven't we been able to move this dial further? Here's my humble opinion after observing several companies across multiple countries.

Reliance on the Handful of Engaged Employees

These are your 'go-to' people for everything. They get things done – your projects, initiatives, fixing daily chaos. However, the issue is that there's not enough capacity in this group to get everything done, like the scenario Jim found himself in. Also, this group tends to be stretched, exhausted and overwhelmed. So, if we don't change things around soon, we could either lose this group to another employer or they could become disengaged or worse, actively disengaged.

Focusing on Disarming the Actively Disengaged

Based on the Gallup graphs above, the increase to the 'engaged group' has predominantly come from reducing the 'actively disengaged group'. So, we've been working really hard to win over the hardest, most opinionated, most stubborn, ungrateful group of employees. It takes a lot of effort and 'hard yakka', as we call it here in Australia. These are the people who make you feel like your life's energy has been sucked out of you when you sit next to them in the canteen

– the energy vampires. So, I agree that reducing the 'noise' from this group is advantageous, but at what cost? Your return on the investment of your personal energy units, the bang for your buck, is not great. This is where we go wrong. We've been trying to disarm the rebellion group. It's a bit like giving too much attention to your child who's throwing a tantrum to calm them down. Sometimes, just leaving them alone for a few minutes works wonders!

Ineffective Drivers

When focusing on the factors to move the needle on engagement, even Gallup has missed an obvious point: involvement. As I've perused their website and articles, I've come across the following four factors that they suggest contribute to improving engagement: purpose; development; a caring manager; and ongoing conversations and focusing on strengths. Let's break these down to gauge their effectiveness.

i. **Purpose:** Simon Sinek (global thought leader on business leadership, TED speaker and best-selling author) has an excellent pragmatic framework, 'Start with why'. This helps us to connect organisational purpose with our employees in an inspiring way. However, unless we get the individuals connected with this purpose through activities and initiatives, it just ends up being another poster on the wall or a slide for your head-office presentation.

ii. **Development:** We send employees on personal and professional development courses, but this generally helps to advance the careers of the already engaged employees. The quiet ones, the disengaged ones, usually don't get a lot of attention – the middle child syndrome, if we can call it that.

iii. **Caring manager:** Yes, a caring manager significantly reduces the employee turnover rate. The issue with this is that we think it is up to the manager or the HR department to engage employees, which puts the accountability on a single individual or department.

iv. **Ongoing conversations and focusing on strengths:** These are essential elements, but we've missed the point about getting people involved. Providing opportunities to raise concerns or improvement ideas without following through doesn't drive engagement. In fact, it works in the opposite direction: employees get frustrated that management hasn't done anything about their ideas or has rejected them without reason. If you don't have systems and processes to capture ideas, collate, prioritise and execute them, you're better off not asking employees for improvement ideas at all. Having ongoing conversations with employees alone is not enough; getting them involved in solving those issues with their input is what drives engagement.

Over Reliance on Capital Expenditure

As leaders, we take on the entire responsibility to look at every piece of new equipment or technology showcased in every trade show around the world to improve productivity. We look for apps, software, scanners, anything to make our workplace 'smart with technology'. After all, we're in the Industry 4.0 era, and with its premise of connecting everything to anything, we should be able to fix a lot of issues right? Yes, we can spend our CapEx (capital expenditure) budget looking for silver bullets, but in my experience, we are trying to implement solutions for the surface-level problem. Employees are quick to critique machinery, equipment and systems, particularly the actively disengaged employees. In addition, if you try to upgrade everything that's needed for your strategic growth

> Employees are quick to critique machinery, equipment and systems, particularly the actively disengaged employees.

initiatives and your employees' wish list, I reckon you will need to 10x your CapEx budget.

Engagement as an Outcome NOT an Activity

We focus on fixing broken things, improving the canteen facilities, or having town hall sessions just when the engagement surveys are around the corner. We can't use engagement as a sporadic activity or an input to drive the scores. Engagement is the outcome you get based on the way you work, getting people involved to continuously improve. Like I learnt in my very first role way back in 1997, reducing employee frustrations naturally leads to high-performance teams where productivity increases at a rapid rate. When you measure that, you won't be surprised to find that engagement is also improving.

We've Missed the Obvious

While you've been busy digging for oil in harsh, difficult conditions, you've missed the diamonds under your feet. The Gallup graph on page 5 clearly shows that the increase to the 'engaged group' has mainly come from reducing the 'actively disengaged group'. This means the disengaged group has relatively flatlined. Yes, the global trend shows a downward path for this disengaged group, but that's largely due to one significant high point of 68% in 2014 (not sure, what was going on back in 2013!). Globally, we've more or less ended up back where we started.

> To put it bluntly, we've got 60% of our global workforce disengaged (the quiet quitters) and we haven't focused on this group to increase engagement and, more importantly, drive productivity.

To put it bluntly, we've got 60% of our global workforce disengaged (the quiet quitters) and we haven't focused on this group to increase engagement and, more importantly, drive productivity. And we know the full impact of this: it is costing the global economy US$8.8 trillion, or 9% of global GDP.

No matter which way you look at it – engagement scores, lost profitability, reduced capacity – there is potential to get a lot more from your business than you've ever thought possible. It's time we focused on the disengaged quiet quitters to unlock this latent capacity. And it's far easier than you think.

Our politicians do it all the time: working on the marginal seats. We know there have been great political victories in the past leveraging this thinking.

In the 1997 UK general election, Tony Blair's 'New Labour' platform and focus on education secured 418 seats, marking an unprecedented swing. The shift ended 18 years of Conservative rule, with Labour gaining 146 seats and reshaping the political landscape.

The 2008 US presidential election witnessed Barack Obama's strategic grassroots efforts, which won 365 electoral votes to John McCain's 173. Obama's social media dominance and message of hope signalled a Democratic shift in leadership.

Australia's 2007 federal election featured Kevin Rudd's victorious 'Kevin 07' campaign, bringing an end to an 11-year reign for then-prime minister John Howard. At this election, Labor secured 83 seats, a pivotal swing, with Rudd's emphasis on climate change action, digital education for children and opposition to WorkChoices appealing to voters and reshaping the political landscape.

Now, let me be clear. I'm not saying that you need to develop a massive publicity campaign to win the hearts and minds of your disengaged employees. I'm not asking you to go out there and start massive town hall sessions and provide empty promises like most politicians do. I've provided these historic political events as metaphors to prove the power of the approach of moving the middle. The group we had all forgotten about. The middle child that gets very little attention.

It's time we focused on them.

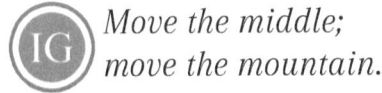
*Move the middle;
move the mountain.*

The UNLOCK Method and Framework

On 20 July 1997, Captain Michael Abrashoff took command of USS *Benfold* – one of the latest and most advanced battle ships of the US Navy. Despite the impressive build, technology and combat prowess, it had two major issues: extremely poor team performance and a demoralised crew.

Even within the highly hierarchical command-and-control US Naval management system, Captain Abrashoff was able to change this situation using the following key principles.

Leveraging Trust

Abrashoff embarked by systematically breaking down the traditional barriers between the captain and crew. He introduced an open-door policy, encouraging sailors to voice concerns and ideas. This move was pivotal; it was not just about listening, but actively incorporating feedback into decision-making. For instance, when a sailor suggested a new method for maintaining the ship's inventory, leading to a 20% reduction in time spent on this task, it was a tangible demonstration of trust in action.

Achieving Quick Results

Abrashoff focused on areas where immediate improvements could be made, demonstrating to the crew that change was not only possible, but happening. One of his early initiatives was improving the ship's operational readiness. Through streamlined processes and efficient resource management, the USS *Benfold* reduced its operational costs by 25% while improving its combat readiness score to above 95% – an unprecedented achievement. Moreover, by turning training exercises, which were often viewed as mundane, into exciting challenges, he not only enhanced skills, but also infused a sense of competition and fun.

Building Ownership

The most transformative aspect of Abrashoff's leadership was how he instilled a sense of ownership in every crew member. He believed that empowering sailors to make decisions and take responsibility would lead to greater investment in the ship's success. This principle was put to the test when he allowed junior sailors to lead complex training exercises, a task traditionally reserved for senior officers. The result was a dramatic increase in the crew's engagement and competence. Abrashoff had a simple rule: If the decision had the potential to kill or injure someone, waste taxpayer's money or damage the ship, it would be his call; for everything else, the crew was in charge.

There were many impressive results under Abrashoff's 20-month command. To name a few: improvements proposed and implemented by the crew increased by 300%; the rate of promotions among *Benfold* sailors became twice that of the navy's average; and retention rates – a critical metric in the navy – rose from a below average 28% to an impressive 100%.

Above all, the following incident highlights the essence of the ship's performance and morale turnaround. The USS *Benfold* earned numerous awards, including the Spokane Trophy, in just seven months under Captain Abrashoff. It was an award established in 1908 by President Theodore Roosevelt, and given annually to the most combat-ready ship in the Pacific Fleet. The commodore, Abrashoff's boss, emailed him congratulating him for the award, but the email contained a caveat. The commodore's ship had won the equivalent award in the Atlantic Fleet plus the navy's all time highest gunnery score of 103.6 (out of 105).

'Until USS *Benfold* can beat that score, I don't want to hear any crowing', the commodore's email read.

Two weeks later, it was USS *Benfold*'s turn. Captain Abrashaoff, without saying a word to his crew, taped a printout of the email to the gun mount. They achieved 104.4 (out of 105), setting a new record. Captain Abrashoff writes in his *New York Times* best-selling book *It's Your Ship,* 'afterwards, I let my crew respond to the commodore. I didn't read it, but I have the impression that they crowed quite a bit.'

The UNLOCK Philosophy

The concept I'm proposing is simple: ignore the actively disengaged, and leverage the engaged few to work on the middle, the disengaged group (the quiet quitters) to grow the engaged percentage. Believe me, the disengaged group is only seemingly disengaged; they are dying to move into the engaged category. If you work with the UNLOCK Method, I'd be surprised if you don't get landslide victories of productivity and engagement improvements, similar to what Captain Abrashoff was able to achieve with USS *Benfold*.

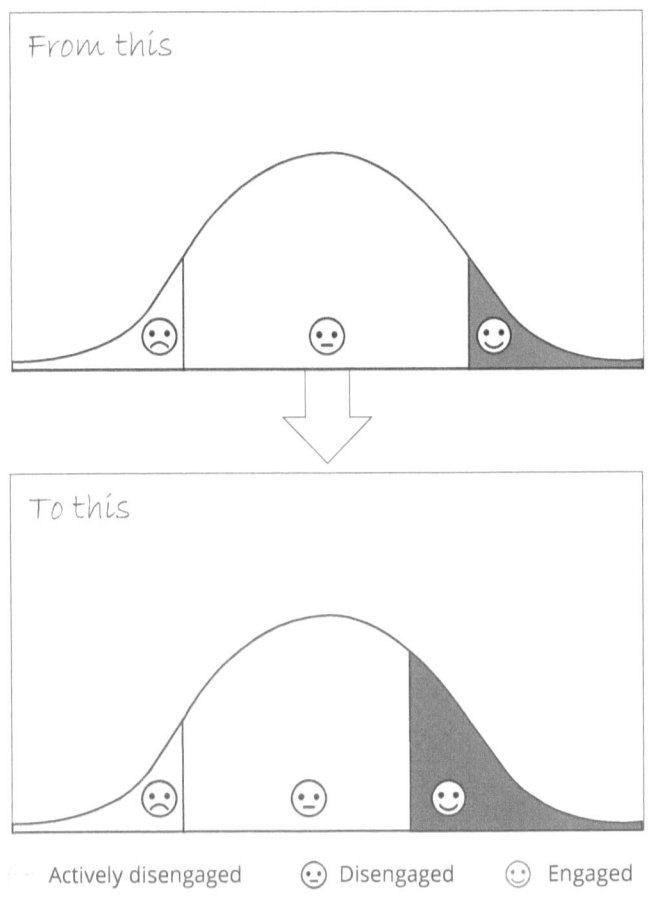

Figure 2: UNLOCK philosophy converting your seemingly disengaged workforce.

The UNLOCK Framework

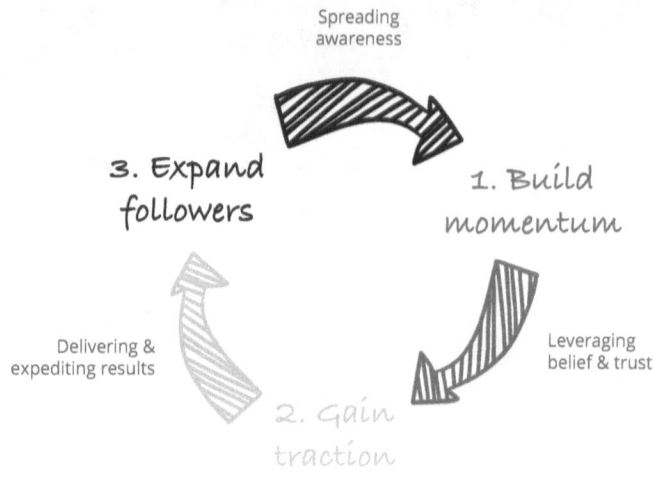

Figure 3: The UNLOCK Framework.

We start (Step 1) with the already engaged few to lead some key projects. Nothing new there, I know. The primary focus is to build momentum, leveraging the trust and belief of your few loyal soldiers. A key point to bear in mind is you need to include a number of carefully chosen individuals from the middle, the disengaged category, in these projects. These individuals are our marginal seats, using the political metaphor from page 12. The key point here is active involvement. Not just passive inclusion in part of a team. Why?

Because Step 2 is about gaining traction. Progress is infectious and exciting. We can't have people who slow us down.

> Employees tend to trust more when they hear the changes from their own.

We want to turn things around quicky, where people start to notice the difference. The tone of the conversations during your shift meetings will change. There will be more smiles and nods from people in the canteen during tea breaks and lunch as you walk by.

Finally, we want to get more followers in Step 3. More believers. More people who are willing to trust that we are changing for the better. We can only do that by spreading the awareness through project team members themselves. Not you. Employees tend to trust more when they hear the changes from their own. A few will change their position.

The cycle then continues by asking the newly converted engaged employees to lead initiatives with a few more carefully chosen disengaged employees in their teams. You will realise that it is easy to generate interest, excitement and momentum. Your task then will be to guide these groups carefully on what projects and initiatives to work on – which is strategy deployment and continuous improvement. This is the work that you should be working on as leader – leading the organisation! However, up until now, you haven't been able to focus on that as you haven't had the bandwidth to execute your brilliant plans. You now can.

It's time to move the middle, move the mountain, and deliver exceptional results.

STEP 1
BUILD MOMENTUM

*'You don't have to be great to start,
but you have to start to be great.'*

– Zig Ziglar

In the middle of the Great Depression, a story of extraordinary resilience and determination began to unfold. This story has now been turned into a movie titled *The Boys in the Boat*. Directed by George Clooney, and based on the book of the same name by Daniel James Brown, this is not just a tale of athletic triumph, but a profound demonstration of the power of taking the first few difficult steps towards a seemingly impossible goal.

It follows the story of the University of Washington's rowing team, most of whom came from humble backgrounds. University rowing is traditionally dominated by the elite, and this group of young men, each carrying their own burdens and dreams, became united by a singular vision – to challenge the status quo and achieve something remarkable by winning gold at the 1936 Berlin Olympics.

Every early morning practice, which was a gruelling session on the cold waters of Lake Washington, was a step towards their audacious goal. The team's journey was built on small victories — a successful row, a harmonious team rhythm, a hard-earned win in a local regatta. These initial triumphs, though small, were crucial — they fuelled the belief that even the most formidable challenges can be overcome.

As the 1936 Berlin Olympics approached, their quest took on a new direction. At a time when the world

> The initial triumphs, though small, were crucial – they fuelled the belief that even the most formidable challenges can be overcome.

was on the brink of war, their pursuit extended beyond sports. The team, representing a nation struggling with economic despair and political turmoil, became a beacon of hope, an embodiment of the American spirit of resilience and unity.

The climax of their journey, the Olympic race, is a testament to the power of those initial steps taken years before. The University of Washington crew, now a finely tuned machine, faced its ultimate challenge. Beset by overwhelming odds, they were rowing not just for victory, but for something much greater — a symbol of hope and determination in a world darkened by adversity.

On 14 August 1936, under the watchful eyes of over 70,000 spectators, including Adolf Hitler, the team faced an unprecedented challenge in their final race. They were positioned in the least favourable lane and initially fell behind when they didn't hear the starting instructions. Despite that disadvantaged start, (spoiler alert) they won the race by the slimmest of margins.

Their triumph is a victory not just for themselves, but for everyone who believes that most difficult challenges can be met with courage, unity and the relentless pursuit of a shared dream. The *Boys in the Boat* is more than a story of winning gold; it's about the strength that comes from taking those initial few steps, however daunting they may be.

Starting the Fire

During my school years back in Sri Lanka, I took part in scouting and basketball as extracurricular activities. At the age of 16, four of my closest scouting friends and I decided to go on a major hiking and personal camping trip for a week – on our own, just the boys. To this day, I'm surprised and grateful that my parents (and the parents of the other lads) allowed us to travel to this remote location on our own, way before mobile phones, Google maps and convenience stores.

The trip was to camp at Horton Plains – a beautiful and unique landscape at the highest tableland in Sri Lanka, with an altitude of 2100 meters above sea level and spreading across more than 3169 hectares. It was later declared a UNESCO World Heritage Site due to the large number of endemic flora and fauna species.

Getting there was a challenge itself. We travelled overnight on a 10-hour train ride, carrying all the gear, tents, food, cooking utensils, first aid equipment etc., and arriving at the Ohiya railway station around 6am. Then we were on foot, literally hacking our way through the jungle for nearly seven hours to arrive at our camping site. I recall getting there in the afternoon and we were totally buggered. Dropping our gear and equipment at the camp site, we just collapsed, ate something out of cans and rested.

Soon, the clouds set in and the temperature started to drop. So, we sprang back to our feet to set up camp. A couple of boys went to collect firewood, while the others attended to the tents, prepared dinner and collected water from the nearby stream. That evening and, in fact, every evening, we built a fire to keep warm, to cook and to keep any wildlife away.

Building that campfire wasn't easy – the firewood was damp due to the high moisture in the area. We could've poured some kerosine over it to get it going, but we had just enough oil for a couple of lanterns for the week.

So, first, we prepared the area and created a fire ring with stones and rocks gathered from nearby surroundings. Then we built cones with some small branches and twigs that were somewhat dry. We then placed dry leaves for kindling inside the cone and tried to light it the old-fashioned way with matchsticks – we didn't have fire-lighter cubes back then. It was a struggle as even the leaves weren't dry enough to catch the fire immediately. Then one of the boys had a brilliant idea – there was plenty of high grass everywhere that we could use as kindling. Once we placed the grass at the bottom and on top of the cone, with the leaves in the middle of the cone, magic happened. We created a fire. We worked with it carefully, placing more twigs and grass, protecting it from the wind to keep the fire going.

At one stage, the flame nearly died, and we managed to resuscitate it by fanning it. Soon afterwards, I remember the wind turning direction and blowing smoke into our eyes. Nevertheless, we got the twigs to catch fire. Yay!

Starting your journey in your own organisation with your big change program is similar to what we went through in building this small fire. In this section, Step 1 – Build Momentum, we will explore how to leverage the belief and trust of a few engaged employees, your kindling, to fan your program to gain momentum.

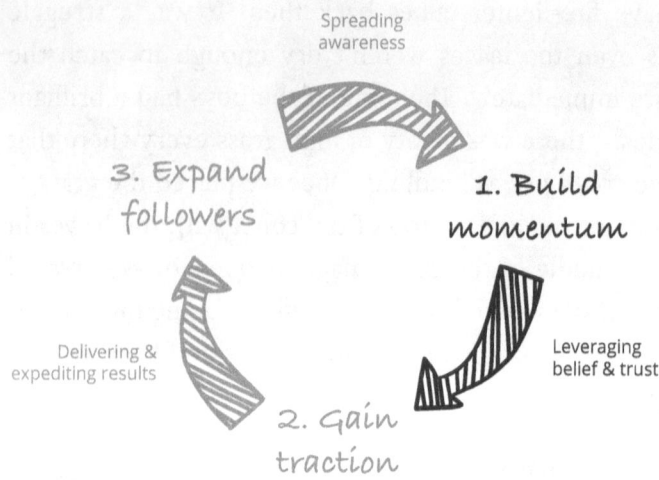

Figure 4: UNLOCK Framework Step 1 – Build momentum.

The three concepts that we will explore in this step are:

Chapter 1: Value Your Values

Demonstrate what you value, and connect with your teams and employees at a human level. Show that you really care. Follow-up with actions and engagement will shift. We learn how this concept was embraced with great success in the very early days of Cadbury chocolate.

Chapter 2: Believe in Them

Aligning with the few diligent soldiers and allies you've got is your only option to build momentum. However, as the leader, you will need to offer generous amounts of mentoring and coaching for these individuals, who may not have enough will power, belief, knowledge or experience to make the initial steps as successful as we need them to be. If we fail here, then we jeopardise the whole journey and fuel the actively disengaged group: 'I told you so. It cannot be done.' We learn from Bill Campbell, a name little known outside of the Silicon Valley C-Suite, on how he coached the big names we are all too familiar with to deliver in excess of a trillion dollars through his coaching.

Chapter 3: What's Your Side Hustle?

There are many individuals in your team/organisation whom you can leverage. As you start building momentum, you will need a few more than your regular go-to individuals who are generally stretched, exhausted and burnt out. So, who are these extra leaders and how do you find them? The secret is to look to your employees' alternative strengths. Sir Brian May, the lead guitarist of the rock band Queen, used his non-musical skill to create simple rhythms for songs, such as 'We Will Rock You'.

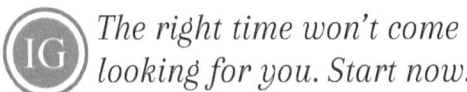

The right time won't come looking for you. Start now.

CHAPTER 1

Value Your Values

*'Our lives begin to end the
day we become silent about
things that matter.'*

– Martin Luther King Jr

We finally reached Kalaburagi after driving for nearly four hours through the semi-arid state of Karnataka in India. Kalaburagi (also known as Gulbarga) has a rich history dating back to medieval times. Initially part of the Hindu kingdom, it flourished under the Bahmani Sultanate as the first capital in the 16th century, showcasing a blend of Persian and local cultures. The city later experienced Mughal and Maratha influences, before becoming part of the British-administered state of Hyderabad. Post-independence, it joined Karnataka in 1956, growing as an educational and industrial hub.

I enjoy such drives into remote parts of the country as it shows the real India – the pace is slower, the people are friendlier, the history is richer, and I reckon the cuisine is purer (and yummier). I guess you could say the same about most countries once you start travelling into the countryside. I've got many recipes from chefs and cooks from these remote parts during my travels, and I could even write a food guide to India... but I digress.

I wasn't holidaying in India nor was I travelling for a gastronomic adventure. I was travelling with the global and the local teams of a multinational alcohol distilling business to their Kalaburagi site to assist them in deploying their global operational excellence program. This was the fifth site in the strategic India-wide roll-out plan, and we were to spend an entire week with the site leadership team.

The distillery was a two-year-old factory in a new industrial estate, and we were treated warmly by the site director, Balaji. It was an impressive site: approximately 150 employees working on three semi-automated lines in the bottling area and a blending area. Over the coming days, I could see that Balaji was the type of leader who cared for everyone, was passionate about the site, and proud about the state and country he lived in.

> Most employees who work at the Gulbarga site leave their families in their hometowns and live as bachelors during the week – they call themselves 'forced-bachelors'.

Given the remoteness of this site, Balaji could not recruit all his employees from the local area. Therefore, he was forced to bring talent from other states and cities, inspiring them to join him on a journey to build a great site. Most employees who work at the Gulbarga site, including Balaji himself, leave their families in their hometowns and live as bachelors during the week – they call themselves 'forced-bachelors', but this helps to bring the team closer. This is also a reason why Balaji takes extra care to look after his team like his own family.

Balaji cared for everyone: he took time to explain the significance of the area; had gone to the trouble of finding the best meals he could afford to be offered at the employee cafeteria; organised a couple of evening meals at a local venue, not only for the visitors, but also for his leadership team and their direct reports to come and enjoy. Balaji's view was that it allowed his extended leadership team to interact with the visitors and understand more about the world outside of this small town. He organised some games for us, along with some delicious meals. He had also organised a small tree for each of the visitors to plant on his site, commemorating the global program kick-off. When he found out that I enjoyed pomegranate fruit (which was not so common in Australia back then), he went out of his way to source them for me to enjoy during the stay.

On the third day of our week, we were going through the process of selecting the initial improvement projects. His team had done their homework and presented us with the potential opportunities based on the last 12 months' performance and the next three years' business needs. I was by the whiteboard going through the list of projects and helping the team to prioritise and finalise the initial projects. We chose three 'no-brainer' projects relating to typical wastes, such as machine stoppages, product waste and throughput increases.

I asked the site leadership to review this list and wanted to ensure that they were happy with the projects – reminding them of two key factors: 1) this is only the start, therefore, we don't have to try and fix everything in the first quarter; and 2) we need to ensure that these projects resonate with the employees. These cannot be strategic projects that only the leadership team are concerned about. The initial projects need to be issues, problems and frustrations that the employees would care about. Then something magical happened.

> The initial projects need to be issues, problems and frustrations that the employees would care about.

Balaji was staring at the board from the back of the room, reclining with his hands behind his head. Suddenly, he sprung out of his chair and came to the board. He took the marker out of my hand, crossed off the third project and highlighted another project that was not an obvious choice.

Reducing water wastage was the project he highlighted. It was way down the list because the total amount wasted was very little, meaning the opportunity from a monetary perspective was not significant. However, Balaji want his team to work on this as one of the initial projects.

I didn't understand his move as it wasn't a big problem for the site or a major frustration for the operators. 'What's your logic, Balaji?' I asked, suspecting many others also wanted to ask the same thing, judging by the expressions on their faces.

Balaji explained, 'You see Ishan, Gulbarga is in a semi-dry area within the state of Karnataka. Some parts of the state receive abundant rainfall from monsoons, but interior areas like Gulbarga face dry conditions. So, water is scarce. Most of the local employees' homes don't have running water. Their wives [most operators were males] walk for several miles, sometimes with young children, to carry water back to their homes. People do whatever they can at home to save water and reduce the extra workload for their loved ones.'

Balaji waited for a few seconds to ensure we understood this point first. The visitors who had travelled from developed countries took a bit more time to fully comprehend this, given the availability of running water even in the most remote parts of their countries.

As I grew up in Sri Lanka, which is also a developing country, I could easily understand what Balaji meant.

He continued with one of the most profound statements I've heard a leader say. 'One of our company values talks about social and environmental responsibility. We have it painted on walls and shown on slides at town hall meetings, and we certainly do whatever we can. I want to work on this project not because of the monetary value, but as a way of demonstrating that we, at Gulbarga site, understand the importance of it and continue to work on it, doing our part. This project will demonstrate that we value our values.'

The hair on the back of my neck stood up and I held the space in the room for everyone to understand the significance of Balaji's thinking. The soft-spoken man who was just over 5 foot appeared a 6-foot powerhouse in my eyes. This is true leadership.

In keeping up with Balaji over the next few weeks and months, I was not surprised to hear that the teams had actually saved a lot more than they estimated. What are the chances of seemingly disengaged people volunteering to be part of a project team in the following quarter? When they've got leaders like Balaji who care for them, the chances are high.

With a global operational excellence program and

leaders like Balaji, it is not surprising that this company regularly gets ranked as one of top 25 supply chains in the world.

Valuing our values and caring for employees is not a new concept. In the late 19th century, amid the industrial turmoil of Victorian England, the Cadbury brothers demonstrated great care and empathy for their factory workers.

A 'Sweet' Vision

In 1824, John Cadbury commenced trading tea and coffee in Birmingham, diversifying into cocoa products by 1831. Due to his age and deteriorating health, he stepped back and his sons George and Richard took over, forming Cadbury Brothers Limited in 1861. They focused on drinking chocolate products, but it was not as successful as they would've liked, mainly due to their inability to extract good quality chocolate from cocoa.

> Valuing our values and caring for employees is not a new concept.

The brothers' tireless efforts took George to Holland to learn from the best how to remove unpleasant fats from cocoa. The result was a pivotal shift in 1866, with the introduction of a new product called 'Pure Cocoa Essence' with the slogan 'Absolutely Pure, Therefore

Best'. This fuelled the company's growth and saved them from the financial disaster they'd been facing.

However, the inner-city factory's conditions contradicted the 'Absolutely Pure' image, which bothered the Cadbury brothers. So, in 1878, George Cadbury was keen to find an innovative solution to the small factory space problem that didn't support the company's growth plan. He purchased a 14.5-acre greenfield site in Worcestershire to build a new factory, 6 kilometres southwest of their Birmingham factory. This move allowed Cadbury Brothers Limited to present their products as pure and with the image of being produced in a healthy environment. Not so radical and innovative so far, just moving the factory.

> He wanted every employee to have a house with a large garden, not be surrounded by factory buildings that prevent the enjoyment of sun, light and fresh air.

With the continual growth of the business, it needed more employees. George knew that eventually the factory surroundings would become built up with high-density terrace houses, creating the same environment that prompted them to move out of Birmingham in the first place. So, in 1893, he privately acquired 140 acres surrounding the factory to maintain a wholesome environment to house his workers. He wanted every employee to have a house with a large garden, not be surrounded by factory buildings, so they could enjoy sun, light and fresh air.

Between 1896 and 1900, George Cadbury built and released 143 houses on 999-year leases. Houses were sold at cost price plus a 4% return, and mortgages were provided at low interest rates. In 1898, acknowledging that not all employees could purchase property, Cadbury constructed 227 smaller houses for rent.

There isn't a lot of information on employee engagement levels after the move to the new factory and the introduction of affordable housing. One could only assume that it provided a supportive network for the children and partners at home.

By the way, George Cadbury named his model town 'Bournville', after a nearby river and the French word for town, 'ville'. You may be familiar with Cadbury's drinking hot chocolate powder product 'Bournville', still in use today.

Motivating Beyond Shareholder Return

When discussing employee engagement, an excellent book that comes to mind is *Drive: The Surprising*

Truth About What Motivates Us by Daniel H Pink. It challenges conventional thinking about motivation and presents a fresh perspective on what drives human behaviour. Pink argues that traditional carrot-and-stick approaches to motivation, based on external rewards and punishments, are often ineffective and even counterproductive. Instead, he advocates for a new paradigm of motivation rooted in intrinsic factors.

Pink introduces the following three fundamental elements of intrinsic motivation:

1. Autonomy: Pink argues that people have an innate desire to be self-directed and have control over their work. When individuals have the autonomy to make decisions and choose how to approach tasks, they are more engaged and motivated. Pink provides real-world examples, such as Google's '20% time' policy, where employees are encouraged to spend 20% of their work hours on personal projects, showcasing the power of autonomy in fostering creativity and motivation.

2. Mastery: Pink contends that humans are driven by the pursuit of mastery and the desire to become better at something that matters to them. When individuals have the opportunity to continually improve their skills and knowledge, they experience a sense of accomplishment and motivation.

3. Purpose: Pink emphasises the importance of connecting work to a larger purpose or cause. When individuals understand how their efforts contribute to something meaningful, they are more engaged and committed. Pink discusses organisations like TOMS Shoes, where the mission to provide shoes to children in need has deeply resonated with both employees and customers.

Throughout *Drive*, Pink emphasises that these intrinsic motivators are more effective than external rewards in fostering engagement and performance. He argues that businesses and organisations can tap into these principles to create workplaces where people are genuinely motivated.

All organisations want to increase their financial performance year on year. What the UNLOCK Method is demonstrating is that there's an easier (and better) way to do this by engaging and involving your employees. This first chapter has explored how

> All organisations want to increase their financial performance year on year. What the UNLOCK Method is demonstrating is that there's an easier way to do this by engaging and involving your employees.

best to start such a journey, especially in situations where employees have lost trust due to our failed attempts or undelivered commitments in the past.

So, find issues that people care about, that would make a significant difference to their work, that communicate that, this time, it's different. It will be slow to kick off, but as you gain momentum, you will unleash unimaginable potential, capacity, capability and profitability.

The book *Firms of Endearment*, by Rajendra Sisodia, Jagdish Sheth and David Wolfe, presents a compelling analysis of this notion. According to the authors, firms of endearment operate beyond just focusing on shareholder wealth. They strive to endear themselves across multiple stakeholder groups (customers, employees, partners, communities and shareholders), and work in a way so that no single stakeholder category wins at the expense of another. Over a 15-year period, these 'firms of endearment' outperformed the S&P 500 14 times, and those companies were featured in Jim Collins's *Good to Great* six times. This remarkable performance underscores the book's premise that companies focusing on broader goals, such as social values, can achieve superior financial success compared with those that don't.

Perhaps you've got some ideas on where to start your business' transformational journey – that area of your workplace that's been the worst performer holding back growth? The machine that's keeping you up all night due to its unreliability? The product that generates more scrap than finished goods? Such issues are easy to find. The question then becomes, how do you fix those issues and, most importantly, who's going to lead the solutions to those issues? You certainly don't have time.

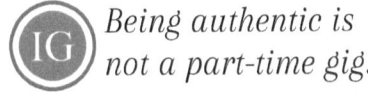 *Being authentic is not a part-time gig.*

CHAPTER 2

Believe in Them

*'We do not need magic to transform
our world. We carry all of the power
we need inside ourselves already.'*

– J.K. Rowling

I remember his first words following a firm handshake, 'Hi Ishan, I'm Arvind. If you ever need anything done from this team, just let me know.' I don't know why, but something told me that he was different.

I had just been promoted as a manufacturing manager to the Arnott's Brisbane site and I flew up from Sydney for a quick two-day visit to meet my new team. With seven large manufacturing lines that had a high degree of complexity and about 600 employees, the Brisbane factory was the biggest site for Arnott's Biscuits. Arvind had already worked his way up to the position of technical support lead for the line I had just taken over. There were only a handful of technical support leads for the entire factory as it required a high degree of technical proficiency and leadership skills to deal with the day-to-day issues on the line or area that one was assigned to.

During my visit, I found that the day shift team leader, who was extremely experienced on that line, had temporarily stepped up as the acting manufacturing manager to hold the fort until I got there. And Arvind had stepped up as the acting day shift leader. I kept this structure going for the first couple of months after I got there, just to give me time to settle in and work out my plan.

Arvind was keen to learn and further progress his career. He shared his personal and professional goals and asked if I would mentor him. I was happy to help in any way I could. Arvind had relocated to Australia with his wife, four-year-old son and only a few hundred dollars back in 2001. It was his eighth year at Arnott's when I met him in 2009.

Arvind often came in early or stayed back after work to have lengthy coaching sessions with me. We spoke about the many facets of leadership from philosophical and practical viewpoints. He soaked everything up like a sponge. He wasn't scared to try new tactics and approaches. He was instrumental in meeting the needs of all three shifts to the best of his ability – even turning up in the middle of the night if machines didn't behave the way they were supposed to.

> We continued our one-on-one coaching sessions and, over the next few months, the transformation that unfolded in front of my eyes was truly remarkable.

Almost everyone on site, no matter whether they were from the leadership team, operators from other lines or casual staff, respected Arvind and knew him for his technical and people skills. He knew each person in that factory – not just about their technical capabilities, which was essential when playing the chess game of who got moved on to which machine, particularly when there was absenteeism, but also their personal circumstances. He knew who had issues outside of work and how he could make them feel better at work.

We continued our one-on-one coaching sessions and, over the next few months, the transformation that unfolded in front of my eyes was truly remarkable. Whether it was his ability to coach his team members, facilitate problem-solving projects or cost-savings initiatives, or think strategically, I was truly inspired by his enthusiasm, drive and commitment. When our line won the 'Line of the Year' award from the chief supply officer for our contribution in 2009, I knew that Arvind had played a key role in that.

When a permanent team leader role opened on day shift, I could not think of a better suited candidate than Arvind. I put forward this proposal at one of the site leadership meetings but to my dismay the suggestion was rejected on two grounds: 1) he was only getting the great results he did because he was 'managing his friends' and 2) the company wanted to recruit some fresh blood to challenge the status quo.

I feared the worst – that Arvind would either resign or completely lose interest – but after I shared the bad news, Arvind rose like a true leader and impressed me with another leadership trait – never give up and never lose sight of one's goals! His immediate response was, 'Ishan, tell me what I need to do prove otherwise'. I could only think of one option – move him to another line as an acting team leader and get him to demonstrate how he can weave his magic to increase performance of that team. Both Arvind and the site leadership team accepted the challenge.

A few months later, I had to leave Arnott's for personal reasons and returned to Sydney in 2011. I kept in touch with Arvind and one evening I received a call from him to say that he had just been offered a permanent role as a team leader of that new area. He thanked me profusely and we continued our chats every three or four months. Another year went by, and Arvind called me to share some more exciting news. The plant director had been to the shop floor to shake his hand and announce that he was one of the few leaders who had been awarded with the highest annual performance rating for that year.

By the way, do you want to know Arvind's personal goal that he shared with me during our first one-on-one meeting? He wanted to be in a management role within 10 years of being with the company – and it was exactly in his tenth year that he was awarded the permanent role in 2011.

We need leaders like Arvind to take charge when starting a journey or a major change initiative. Employees on the factory floor, particularly the disengaged ones, tend to listen to and trust leaders like Arvind. These leaders have a way about them that lights people up and recharges them. They also have an unwavering loyalty for the company and for you as the leader, as much as for the team. These are the traits we need to harness and leverage for the first round of disciples. We just need these individuals to trust you and trust the process.

It may be difficult for some to take that leap of faith. Generally, it is because your company, department or the site may have started some sort of major change initiatives in the past with a big bang announcement, promising that things would change, but nothing did. Would that be right? It is quite common for major change initiatives to fail.

As long as you, as the senior leader, is clear of the overall change you're after, ask your disciples to take a few steps with you that they are comfortable in taking. Once they take those few steps, the next few will become clear. It is a bit like driving at night on a major highway at 100 km per hour. You can only see 20 to 30 meters ahead of you, depending on the power of your headlights, yet, you're

> Sometimes, even engaged leaders, despite being loyal to you and the cause, may feel a bit insecure about the change process.

comfortable roaring down the highway in pitch darkness as you know that when you drive the 20 metres in front of you, a further 20 metres will be illuminated. Of course, this happens on a continual loop, but at a microscopic level it is interesting to notice.

Sometimes, even engaged leaders like Arvind, despite being loyal to you and the cause, may feel a bit insecure about the change process. You need to double down on your commitment and stand by the few who are willing to take on the lead role on the first few initiatives – the pilot projects. Like driving down on the highway at speed, ask them to take the first few steps with you.

On a Positive Note

Siaosi, George to his workmates, is one such team leader that I recently came across at a multinational manufacturing factory in Sydney. George hid his reservations and concerns extremely well, but gave his 100% commitment. George has a towering personality and his build as a 6-footer helps him to literally and metaphorically stand tall. However, he doesn't have the typical intimidating alpha male personality. His style exudes confidence, which is his biggest strength. He is soft spoken and often not rushed either in talk or walk. Once you start interacting with George, his personality and confidence is infectious. You cannot help but like him.

When we started the journey at this site, he was the day shift team lead and led one of the two initial improvement projects we kicked off. I was walking with him side-by-side throughout the initial rigorous 12 weeks, and he led that project flawlessly. His team delivered a 35% increase to their capacity-stricken critical line. To this date, this project remains as one of the poster projects for the company's operational excellence program in Australia.

I watched how George led the improvement initiative team meetings week after week. He was humble enough to put his hand up and ask what he should do in preparation for each weekly meeting. He made time for his team members to follow up on the actions so that they would have something positive to report on the following week. For things that needed external expertise, he spoke to the site leader to make things happen. And above all, he joked around, smiled a lot and held the belief for the team that this project will not fail.

Like most improvement initiatives, we don't need a lot of capital to upgrade equipment. The majority of the improvements come from changes to processes and some minor tweaking of equipment. George spoke to the other shifts before making temporary changes permanent, and got the risk assessments done to ensure that the newly introduced changes would not introduce any adverse effects, particularly to operator safety.

At one team meeting, I saw George translate a discussion into Samoan for his team member to help them clearly understand what was being discussed. He patiently listened to that individual's response and translated it back to English for the rest of the team. It is these little nuances that make his team members feel included, involved and listened to. During another meeting, I was surprised that a team member who had taken the day off to look after his sick grandchild had made alternative arrangements for a few hours, so he could drop in for the team meeting – unbelievable!

The team's triumph could not be kept a secret within the company. It started to spread and people within the site could feel that something was happening, changing and improving.

George and the project team presented their progress to the state director and the national operations director. Although George had done some basic PowerPoint presentations, most of the team had not presented to a group before, let alone to senior leaders. They were comfortable and confident in showing what they had achieved by themselves and confidently asked for the national operations director's commitment for additional capital expenditure to further improve the line. The director's response was, 'I have no issues signing off additional capital expenditure when you have tackled all the improvements within your reach. You've done your part and I'll now do mine.'

The national operations director then asked for a favour from this team. He asked if the team would be willing to present at the company's upcoming National Operations Conference. When 75 of the most senior operational leaders in Australia came to this site a couple of months later as part of the conference, George and the team surpassed everyone's expectations!

It was only during a casual chat over a coffee a few weeks after the conference that George confided in me that he initially had doubts about what was being asked of him and his team, however, he didn't share it with anyone. I asked him what kept him going and his response was, 'I couldn't let down my boss. I can see that he's changing things around. If I gave up, my team would too.'

Hollywood actor Tom Cruise is known for being a positive force on movie sets, even in most trying conditions. On a Graham Norton Show episode on BBC One (series 15 episode 9), Tom Cruise and Emily Blunt talk about a challenging experience they had while filming *The Edge of Tomorrow*. Norton teasingly asks Cruise, 'Is it true that Emily Blunt broke your spirits?' Blunt sets the context that it was particularly a hard, hot day where they were filming being dropped out of a large aircraft wearing exo-suits. The movie set had been a tight one with little ventilation and everyone was dripping in sweat under those tough conditions. Blunt looked at Cruise and commented, 'This sucks, Tom!' to which Cruise nodded, took a deep breath and replied, 'It's a challenge'. Cruise laughs on the Norton show and responded, 'You know what? If I start to complain, it's on. It is on!'

Actors like Cruise know that they recharge everyone else. People believe in their belief. If the leader shows any signs of softening, buckling or giving up hope, then you're not going to get even the normal effort, let alone the discretionary effort from your employees. Thank you, George, for being the torchbearer with your insatiable positivity. We could not have asked for more from you.

When picking your disciples to help you lead change, yes, you need to pick the people who'd be willing to come along on the journey with you – people who believe and trust you and, in turn, you believe in them. However, that's not enough – they need to be coachable. With change and transformation journeys, let's not forget that we are predominantly trying to change people's behaviours. That means the outcomes are not predictable. We need to try different approaches with the intention of involving and engaging those who are seemingly disengaged.

So, we need our change leaders, like Arvind and George, to be coachable. How do you know if you've got coachable individuals? Two attributes keep coming up over and over again in many of my research articles – they need to be honest and humble. Based on the trustworthiness of these individuals you are depending on, it is safe to assume that they would be honest; however, they need to be extremely humble as well, putting their team members' interests first. And given that you'd be coaching them, my question to you is, how do you become a great coach?

> How do you know if you've got coachable individuals? They need to be honest and humble.

Before answering that question, let me ask you another one. What do these Silicone Valley Fortune 500 leaders have in common: Steve Jobs (Apple founder), Eric Schmidt (former Google CEO), Jonathan Rosenberg (advisor to Alphabet Inc), Sheryl Sandberg (former chief operating officer of Meta Platforms/Facebook), Sundar Pichai (Google CEO), Sergey Brin and Larry Page (Google co-founders)? The answer is executive coach Bill Campbell who has coached many, many top leaders. So, going back to my previous question of 'how do you coach?', let's learn from one of the greatest: Bill Campbell.

Learning from a Trillion Dollar Coach

Bill Campbell's journey to Silicon Valley fame was different from the stereotypical young genius dropout born to a wealthy influential family. Born in 1940 in Pennsylvania, Campbell was a role model in his youth – a hard-working student excelling academically and in extracurricular activities. His passion for football was evident during his college years at Columbia University where he joined the football team. Despite being smaller than his teammates, his fearless approach and leadership skills earned him the nickname 'Ballsy'. Under his captaincy, Columbia won the Ivy League title in 1961.

After college, Campbell pursued a football coaching career, starting at Boston College and later receiving an offer from Pennsylvania State University. However, he chose to return to Columbia out of loyalty. Unfortunately, he faced challenges due to inadequate resources, which lead to his resignation after a significant loss in 1979.

At age 39, Campbell shifted to the business world, starting at an ad agency then quickly moving to a top position at Kodak. His big break came when John Sculley, a former college friend and then-CEO of Apple, recruited him. This move proved pivotal: Campbell soon became vice president of sales and played a crucial role in launching Apple's first Macintosh computer.

Beyond his business acumen, Campbell became renowned for his mentorship skills, particularly through his close relationship with Steve Jobs. His ability to provide sound advice and creative problem-solving support established him as a valued mentor and business coach in Silicon Valley. His journey from football coach to business mentor showcases his adaptability, leadership and the impact of nurturing professional relationships.

Campbell's first business coach client was Apple, including Jobs himself. Soon the word got out. In 2001, Eric Schmidt had just been offered the CEO role at Google, and he wanted to know who this Bill Campbell was. Campbell spent the next 15 years with the Google

> Known as 'the Coach', Bill Campbell has helped to build some of the greatest tech companies, including Google, Apple and Intuit, and to create in excess of a trillion dollars in market value.

Known as 'the Coach', Bill Campbell has helped to build some of the greatest tech companies, including Google, Apple and Intuit, and to create in excess of a trillion dollars in market value. After his death in 2016, aged 76, his disciples from Google, Eric Schmidt, Jonathan Rosenberg and Alan Eagle, authored the book *Trillian Dollar Coach* to honour their mentor and to offer his wisdom in an essential guide. The book is based on interviews with over 80 people who knew and loved Bill Campbell, along with the authors' personal experiences with him. So, if you're looking for an inspiring coaching book with principles, stories and practical tips, I highly recommend this book, which I've summarised into the following three lessons:

Lesson 1. Lead With Heart: Embrace Emotions and Enhance Performance

Embracing emotional openness in the workplace can significantly enhance employee satisfaction and performance. Campbell, known for his casual and friendly demeanour, often expressed his personality through actions like giving bear hugs and blowing kisses in formal settings. This approach challenges the traditional belief in the business world that showing emotions indicates incompetence or lack of professionalism. If you're familiar with Brené Brown's work in the area of 'leadership vulnerability', you know that emotional openness improves team performance and employee satisfaction.

Leaders like Campbell show that expressing emotions can be a sign of effective leadership, fostering a deeper connection with employees. This personal warmth and informality, as seen in Campbell's unwavering support for colleagues in need, such as his daily hospital visits to Steve Jobs, illustrates the positive impact of emotional engagement. This aligns with the traits of coachability, such as honesty, humility, perseverance and a continuous desire to learn.

Lesson 2. Amplify Ideas: Unlock the Power of Inclusive Decision-making

Bill Campbell's approach in Silicon Valley during the 1980s highlighted the importance of inclusivity and diversity in harnessing top talent, especially in a male-dominated business environment. One notable example was his encouragement of Deb Biondolillo, Apple's head of HR and one of the few women in a leadership role at the time, to take a more prominent position in meetings. By urging her to move from the back to the front of the room, Campbell demonstrated his support for her and his belief in the value of diverse perspectives.

This action was part of Campbell's broader strategy to include more women in decision-making processes, drawing from his sports background where selecting the best players was key. To bring out the best in teams at meetings, he did two things: ensure everyone contributed and pushed beyond consensus.

This approach aligns with Harvard Professor Linda Hill's 'collective genius' concept, emphasising diversity, inclusivity and collaboration. Both advocate for emotionally intelligent leadership that encourages participation from all team members, challenges traditional hierarchies, and values continuous learning. This inclusive approach fosters innovation and effective decision-making by harnessing diverse perspectives. When you can find a spare 17 minutes, perhaps over your next lunch break, watch Linda Hill's TED talk, titled 'How to manage for collective creativity'.

Lesson 3. Foster Trust: Team Growth from Managers to Coaches

Building trust is essential for effective leadership. Campbell earned trust through consistent delivery on promises and by treating people well, which allowed him to influence others significantly, including facilitating Deb Biondolillo's involvement in meetings. Campbell demonstrated trust-building by actively listening and asking questions, a method supported by a 2016 *Harvard Business Review* paper highlighting that great listeners provoke spontaneous insights, which fosters a sense of competence, belonging and autonomy in others.

Trust also plays a critical role in decision-making, as seen in Campbell's time at Intuit. His perspective prevailed during a board deadlock because of the trust he had cultivated, particularly through his attentive and non-judgemental listening style, described as 'free-form listening'. Trust eliminates the distractions of emotional biases and personal conflicts, focusing on the core issues and facilitating honest dialogue.

Such an environment, shaped by trust, is favourable to finding the best solutions through open discussions.

Fabulous learnings from the trillion-dollar coach.

Look Beyond the Façade

This chapter has highlighted the importance of finding the right type of engaged individuals who can help you to start this journey, mission or initiative. We need people who are dedicated, coachable, loyal, diligent, humble, honest and likeable. Seeing this list of leadership traits required, you may be uncertain whether you have such individuals in your workplace. Well, if you're willing to give them your unwavering support, inspiration and time, I can guarantee that you'll be able to find and polish the rough diamonds on your site.

We see this in the movie *The Devil Wears Prada*, where Andy Sachs (played by Anne Hathaway), a recent college graduate, enters the cut-throat fashion industry as an assistant to the formidable Miranda Priestly (played by Meryl Streep), editor-in-chief of a prestigious fashion magazine. Initially troubled by self-doubt and overwhelmed by her demanding role, Andy finds herself in the shadow of her glamorous colleagues. However, Miranda's unwavering standards and tough mentorship become the catalyst for Andy's growth. With determination and grit, Andy learns the ropes, transforms her appearance and attitude, and ultimately thrives in the high-pressure world of fashion.

While your site might not be as glamorous as a prestigious fashion magazine, I bet the demands and the pressures are similar.

You need to find the individuals who are popular amongst your employees. They are easy to find – they are always the caring ones, the ones who organise social events, the ones who try to help people personally, the ones who are there to help the company unselfishly. They may not be your next CEO, they may not be able to climb the corporate ladder, and that's OK. If you are looking for the right candidate to be able to replace you over time *and* lead the teams today *and* have the potential to grow, then you are looking for unicorns.

If you've still got doubts about whether you've got the right calibre of individuals with self-belief, resilience and the readiness to embrace challenges, there may be another option. You may have the right people, but you may not know of their real skills and true potential. Their hidden skills. How do you find the hidden gems?

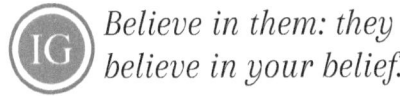

Believe in them: they believe in your belief.

CHAPTER 3

What's Your Side Hustle?

*'When we are no longer
able to change the situation,
we are challenged to
change ourselves.'*

– Viktor Frankl

Mike gulped the last sip of his second cup of coffee (or was it his third?), punched my left arm jokingly while saying, 'Are you ready my friend?' in his strong Kiwi (New Zealand) accent. At 5:45am, Mike, second-in-charge (2IC) for the day shift at a well-known company, was getting ready for the pre-shift team huddle. I'd heard about the great meetings that Mike facilitates, and I wanted to witness it myself.

Wearing my high-visibility jacket, earplugs and safety glasses, I was ready to see how Mike, always the optimist and high-energy leader, would prepare his team of 20-odd people to face whatever the next eight hours would bring. As we walked into the relatively new, brightly lit factory, I immediately saw the high-speed lines running in the background. A short distance ahead of us, I could see the crew had already assembled at their meeting point.

Mike, who looks like actor Gerard Butler, said, 'Good morning team', in a commanding and uplifting tone with a smile on his face. 'We have a visitor today', he said looking at me. I could already feel Mike's positive energy radiating and (metaphorically) waking up the fellow team members at 6am.

I later found out that Mike was relatively new to this company and his story is a compelling tale of resilience and adaptability. Born in New Zealand and raised in

Melbourne, Australia, Mike's journey took him from the bustling streets of Melbourne to the heart of the events industry in the Gold Coast (a Queensland tourist destination), with radiating heat, glaring sunshine, sandy beaches, happy tourists and mega events. He loved working with large groups, fixing technical issues that could potentially be show-stoppers (literally) and the buzz of large crowds. Mike's work was like a swan on a lake – calm and serene on the top while full of adrenaline-driven paddling under water!

In his earlier years, Mike worked for a company that set up stages for massive events, and his hand had once shaken that of Sir Richard Branson.

In early 2020, Mike's life was a whirlwind of excitement and challenges, with work scheduled all the way up to New Year's Eve 2020, leaving him very little spare time. However, the onset of COVID-19 drastically altered his trajectory. Government restrictions swiftly reduced event capacities from 10,000 to zero. By the end of March 2020, Mike found himself at home, his once-packed schedule now hauntingly empty.

Although faced with this unprecedented situation, Mike refused to be controlled by the outside world. He signed up with a labour-hire company, briefly trying his hand at truck driving before realising sitting in a truck by himself for long hours wasn't for him. He then discovered an opportunity at a different site with the same company, not the site I met him at. During his interview, when asked about his motivations, Mike's response was straightforward: he needed money and sought the role that paid the most. So, he was a offered a role on the not-so-highly sought after night shift, which was a win-win for Mike and the company.

He started in a mundane role loading raw material. Mike's restless spirit was not content with monotonous work, so he took it upon himself to learn the operation of the entire line. 'If you watch the security video footage of the factory, you will see a blur moving around the line, like a bee buzzing around. *I am the blur*', Mike told me, sipping his next cup of coffee and smiling. He was troubleshooting everywhere. He was also a leader without a title, helping operators across the line.

Mike's helpful nature, infectious positivity and endless energy soon got the attention of the site leadership team. A couple of roles later, he became the 2IC on day shift at Brisbane's flagship new site.

> Mike's philosophy was simple yet profound: see the positive in everyone, every day and everything.

Mike's philosophy was simple yet profound: see the positive in everyone, every day and everything. This approach became his mantra, guiding his interactions and leadership style. As he stepped into his new role at this manufacturing plant, Mike brought with him not just his previous experiences, but also a unique perspective shaped by the challenges he had faced. He believes that starting the day positively is not just a choice. 'You've got to start the day positive and pump some energy into the team. Hopefully, it will rub off on some', he said playfully.

> You've got to start the day positive and pump some energy into the team. Hopefully, it will rub off on some.

Mike's approach to leadership in the manufacturing environment was unconventional. He infused his experience from the events industry into his new role, emphasising the importance of engagement, teamwork and positivity. His ability to adapt to different situations and bring out the best in his team quickly earned him respect and admiration.

In team meetings, I observed him asking open questions that involved, engaged and motivated the team.

He focused on daily tasks and achievements to foster a sense of accomplishment and belonging. He did this as an elegant dance moving from one end of the semi-circle, created by the team, to the other. Sometimes he moved in closer to the operators and then he moved back closer to the whiteboard, pointing to some metrics that were relevant to the team. I wondered if Mike learnt these moves from showbiz personalities who knew how to draw in their fans on the large stages that Mike once built.

Talking to the team casually after the morning meeting, I could see that Mike was well respected. He'd made a big difference to the team in a short period of time. He went from being a newcomer in the manufacturing world to a respected 2IC, demonstrating that leadership is not just about directing others but about inspiring and engaging them.

Mike is a testament to the human spirit's resilience and adaptability. His story epitomises the quote from Viktor Frankl, a psychologist and Holocaust survivor, 'When we are no longer able to change the situation, we are challenged to change ourselves.'

We can find talent in unusual ways. People like Mike are like rough, unpolished diamonds waiting to be discovered and elevated. These individuals can also potentially lead your change initiatives, improvement projects or even back-fill your ace team leaders to manage the day-to-day while they help you with the initiatives. You've definitely got more individuals with hidden talents than the few you've been working with. It is amazing how hidden talents can actually help people in their primary roles as well.

Rocking with Queen

Sir Brian Harold May's story is a compelling one that demonstrates the power of merging diverse talents. Best known as Queen's lead guitarist (the rock band, not the late Queen Elizabeth II), May's academic pursuit in astrophysics, resulting in a PhD from Imperial College London in 2007, might seem at odds with his musical career, yet this odd combination has enriched his artistic expression.

Astrophysics calls for pattern recognition, problem-solving and creative thinking within scientific parameters. These skills, surprisingly relevant to music, have allowed May to approach his craft with a unique blend of analytical rigour and imaginative flair. This is evident in Queen's iconic tracks like 'We Will Rock You', where simplicity and rhythm have helped deliver a global anthem.

In astrophysics, one must often visualise abstract concepts and translate them into understandable models. With his music, May has demonstrated the ability to conceptualise sound and transform it into audible masterpieces. This has helped to blend complex structures of rock, ballad and opera to produce legendary songs. Freddy Mercury is said to have included the word 'Galileo' into the lyrics of 'Bohemian Rhapsody', honouring May's interests in astrophysics.

May's story serves as a powerful reminder to blend talents, embrace exploration and harmonise passions in pursuit of their unique compositions in life and work. Stepping into uncharted territories, be it in space or in our creative endeavours, can lead to remarkable achievements.

> Stepping into uncharted territories, be it in space or in our creative endeavours, can lead to remarkable achievements.

Aggregate Synergy

As I was researching other real-life stories of individuals who had demonstrated this concept, I came across a movie I had seen nearly a decade ago – *Moneyball,* starring Brad Pitt, based on the book of the same name, by Michael Lewis.

Directed by Bennett Miller, *Moneyball* follows Billy Beane (played by Pitt), the general manager of the Oakland Athletics baseball team. It offers a fascinating lesson in leveraging hidden talents for remarkable success. Beane, with limited resources, used an unconventional approach to build a winning baseball team. He recognised that traditional player evaluation metrics were flawed; instead, he embraced a data-driven analysis method to identify undervalued players who excelled in specific areas, even if they didn't fit the conventional mould.

> There's definitely more capability and talent in your teams than you are aware of, though they may not stand out at first glance.

Billy Beane's remarkable success wasn't just about using data; it was about embracing innovation and leveraging the hidden skill of statistical analysis to disrupt the status quo. His story offers valuable insights into the power of recognising and nurturing unique talents within an organisation. By breaking away from convention and allowing employees to tap into their uncharted abilities, teams can achieve unprecedented success.

We are often overwhelmed and burdened with the lack of talent to take on lead roles as we launch major change initiatives. There's definitely more capability and talent in your teams than you are aware of, though they may not stand out at first glance. Like finding truffles, search for these individuals, dig them out, coach them and deliver value.

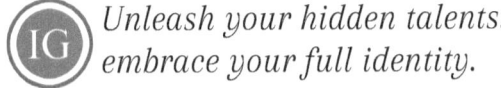 *Unleash your hidden talents: embrace your full identity.*

'The man who moves a mountain begins by carrying away small stones.'

– Confucius

In 1932, carpenter Ole Kirk Kristiansen started producing wooden toys in Denmark. Due to the tough economic conditions, he asked his brothers and sisters to act as guarantors for a loan of DKK 3000. (My rough estimate is that this equates to about US$7500–10,000 in 2024.) A few years later, Kristiansen doubled down and further concentrated on toy production, and wanted a new name to mark this new era. He held a competition among his employees, but it was Kristiansen's entry that won. Kristiansen played with the two Danish words *leg* and *godt* (meaning 'play well') to produce the name LEGO. The new name was officially used from January 1936.

From its humble beginning in 1932 until 1998, LEGO never posted a loss. From 1999 to 2003, LEGO's financial situation deteriorated rapidly. The company's expansion into areas outside of its core business of toy bricks, such as theme parks, video games, clothing and watches, led to increasing costs without the corresponding returns. It had a particularly challenging year in 2003 as it faced a 30% drop in sales and continued to mount big losses.

When the former McKinsey consultant Jørgen Vig Knudstorp joined LEGO as the first non-family CEO in 2004, the company had lost US$300 million that year and reported a total debt of US$800 million. Knudstorp knew that he needed to gain traction quickly to ensure that kids in the future could continue to play with the plastic interlocking blocks that Kristiansen created back in 1949.

One of Knudstorp's first actions was to implement quick-win projects designed to halt LEGO's financial haemorrhage and restore profitability. Recognising the dire need for immediate cash flow, he made the bold decision to streamline the product line, reducing the number of components from 7000 to 3000. This simplification led to significant cost savings and re-emphasised the company's focus on the classic LEGO brick. He named this turn-around journey 'Back to Brick', which helped the company steer away from failed product extensions, like Jack Stone and Gladiator.

> Knudstorp implemented lean management techniques, which improved efficiency, reduced waste and sped up the time-to-market for new products.

Knudstorp also made the strategic decision to sell off non-core assets, including the LEGO theme parks, which, although popular, were draining the company's resources and profitability.

Another critical aspect of the rapid results strategy

was the revamping of LEGO's production and supply chain processes. Knudstorp implemented lean management techniques, which improved efficiency, reduced waste and sped up the time-to-market for new products. These changes not only saved costs, but also enabled LEGO to be more responsive to market trends and consumer demands.

Knudstorp fostered a culture of openness and inclusivity, where ideas and feedback were actively solicited and valued at all levels of the organisation. His inclusive approach was a shift from the top-down management style that had previously been in place. This new participatory culture not only boosted morale, but also unearthed a wealth of creative solutions and concepts, leading to the development of some of LEGO's most successful lines, like LEGO Star Wars and LEGO Harry Potter.

Knudstorp also recognised the importance of empowering his employees. He decentralised decision-making, giving more autonomy to teams and individuals. Employees felt more invested in LEGO's success, leading to increased productivity and a greater commitment to the company's goals.

The financial turnaround was amazing. From a daunting US$300 million loss in 2004 to a striking profit of US$150 million in 2005, and soaring to approximately

US$1 billion by 2013, LEGO's recovery demonstrates the power of engaged employees coupled with focused initiatives delivering rapid results.

Knudstorp's leadership style was key in this paradigm shift. He championed transparency and open dialogue, sharing challenges and victories alike with the entire workforce.

> The key to revival lies in recognising and leveraging the wealth of resources that exist within.

LEGO's journey highlights that the company's turnaround wasn't solely due to executive decisions. It was a collaborative effort by empowered and engaged individuals to share their creativity and ideas. It demonstrates that sometimes the key to revival lies in recognising and leveraging the wealth of resources that exist within, waiting to be tapped and flourished.

Keeping the Flame Burning

You may recall my camping trip as teenager from page 27. We were relieved that we managed to get the initial fire going. This is the danger period as the twigs burn out very quickly. We didn't have many twigs, so we started to scramble. We placed some small dry branches by the fire ring and strategically increased the size of the cone. You cannot rush this stage, unless one has ample dry firewood. It needed so much attention and care to keep the flame going. A couple of times the flame nearly died, but it was relatively easier to fan the flame back to life. After about 15 minutes, and with only a few minutes of daylight left, we finally had some solid firewood burning. With the campfire now roaring and the tents erected, everyone was looking forward to our first camp meal and a good night's sleep.

Similar to how we got the campfire going, in Step 2, the idea is to do exactly that with your change journey in your organisation. Do whatever it takes to keep the flame going.

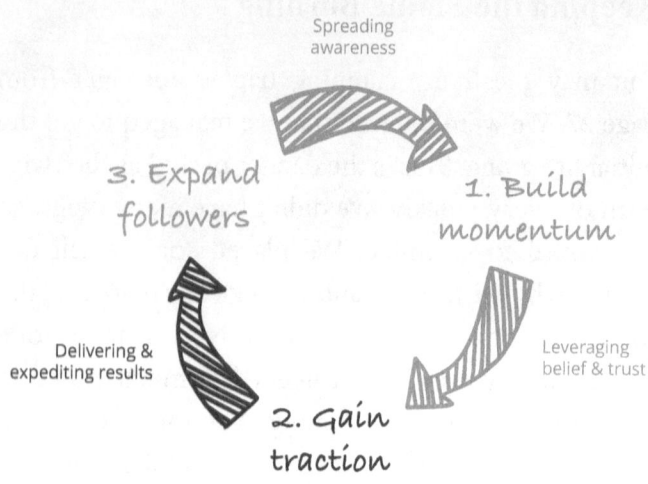

Figure 5: UNLOCK Framework Step 2 – Gain traction.

The following six chapters will explore the six concepts of Step 2 – Gain Traction.

Chapter 4: It's Not Me; it's YOU

Leaders think that majority of employees are not engaged and just turn up in body, and they would be correct and validated by global survey data. The employees, on the other hand, are frustrated that no one is involving them or doing anything about their issues. The fault is not with them. Three Cambridge University friends who started Innocent Drinks have done really well for themselves and the company with this understanding.

Chapter 5: Give it a Go

If we are to involve employees by getting them to volunteer their ideas, we need to get one key factor right in our organisations: culture. You need a culture that encourages, empowers, enables, endorses, embraces and elevates employees (yes, I went through all the E words) to have a crack and learn from mistakes collectively as a team. If they didn't operate with this culture from the beginning, we wouldn't have Google today.

Chapter 6: SMART Factories and DUMB Operators

The world has fallen in love with SMART technology, and we look for silver bullet solutions with Industry 4.0 – apps and the cloud – to solve our problems. At the same time, we are creating DUMB operators – operators who are constantly **D**evalued, **U**nderestimated, **M**isunderstood and **B**elittled. Sadly, they are waiting to be **D**eveloped, **U**tilised, **M**otivated and **B**elieved-in. If we think artificial intelligence is better than natural intelligence, then the end is near. Unfortunately, this thinking has been around for nearly half a century and could've jeopardised the entire Apollo mission at NASA.

Chapter 7: Start with Who

Simon Sinek tells us to 'start with why' and he's right. However, before the 'why', we need to focus on the who. It is important to carefully work out the critical individuals, the 'who' that need to be on board with the inspiring 'why'. We learn that if Walt Disney animation studios didn't think this through carefully, the world would've missed out on *The Lion King* and the very existence of Walt Disney studios.

Chapter 8: Flaws and Fortunes

We know that success seldom comes in a straight line. We may feel that the world is unkind and hasn't dealt us the right cards. Many have created success from their mistakes by failing forward. The humble Post-It® Note that is making billions for 3M would not have seen the light of day if they hadn't embraced their errors and thought about solving the problems to profit.

> Many have created success from their mistakes by failing forward.

Chapter 9: Adapting to Triumph

US President Dwight D Eisenhower is famous for saying, 'In preparing for battle, I have always found that plans are useless, but planning is indispensable'. Across the Atlantic, Winston Churchill said, 'Plans are of little importance, but planning is essential'. We know that often our plans don't materialise exactly the way we want them to in the real world. So, we need to be good at shifting our tack, often on the fly. Luckily, Netflix founders were really good at this, which was essential to their success.

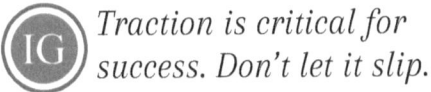 *Traction is critical for success. Don't let it slip.*

CHAPTER 4

It's Not Me; it's You!

*'Yesterday I was clever,
so I wanted to change the world.
Today I am wise, so I am
changing myself.'*

– Rumi

Mike Allen was the supply chain director for Kellogg South Africa and he had a major problem. The supply chain, mainly the manufacturing part, was a major constraint, so much so, that they couldn't manufacture sufficient product volumes to satisfy the demand. The friendly banter from his sales counterpart during executive leadership meetings had been starting to bug him. The factory technically and theoretically had sufficient capacity to make more than enough volume for what sales demanded; however, when all the factory inefficiencies were taken into account, they just couldn't keep up.

This is quite a common phenomenon with most factories around the globe, irrespective of the size or the sector. And in Mike's case, this is the better problem to have as it is easier to reclaim wasted capacity than have a highly efficient factory run out capacity, which would require line extensions, factory extensions or even entirely new factories to be built, depending on the size of the problem.

During my first visit to South Africa in early 2012, we sat down to explore how best I could support Mike and the team. Being a seasoned supply chain leader, Mike knew exactly which levers he needed to pull and his request of me was to help unlock as much capacity as possible for the main cash-cow product, Corn Flakes original.

Specific improvement project teams were set up and Mike found the right people to lead them – those who were engaged and willing to believe in the process. Based on some initial basic data analysis, we knew that the majority of the issues came from the cooking process at the start of the line. This is the part where corn kernels get pressure cooked in large rotating drums, which could hold a metric tonne of corn kernels with ease.

We set up focus groups for most of the operators from all three shifts to contribute to solving this problem. All project leaders were trained on effective brainstorming, and we created a plan to bring in a few operators at a time to explore answers to one specific question: 'Why can't we get 100% from the cookers every day?' The specific steps to structured problem-solving can be found in my previous book, *ADVANCE: 12 Essential Elements to Supercharge Productivity and Profitability*.

> All project leaders were trained on effective brainstorming to explore answers to one specific question: 'Why can't we get 100% every day?'

Sam was a machine whisperer, a gun operator, a true expert on the cookers; however, he hardly spoke out and simply did what was asked of him – nothing more, nothing less. In previous conversations, I'd heard Sam's name being mentioned as someone who has a lot of potential to do more, be more and grow more. Unfortunately, most of those conversations ended up with comments stating that he wasn't interested. Most senior leaders were unhappy about Sam's lack of willingness to take initiative or even be involved in any initiative.

As the project lead conducted the brainstorming session for day shift, I was just sitting at the back, observing. At the end of that session, the participants left the room and I was just standing by the whiteboard going through all the issues raised, when I heard project lead, Gloria, entering the room.

She approached quite hurriedly and as she got closer, I could see that she was almost in tears from a cocktail of emotions. Gripping my arm, she said, 'Ishan, I'm shaking. Sam talked to me as we were walking out. He said that no one for the past 17 years had asked him for his opinion – until now!'

The impact of this moment would not be apparent to me for a few more weeks. The team focused on some of the quick-win issues that were raised through the focus groups. They communicated the fixes and progress through the shift start-up meetings. And when the others saw Sam embracing the changes, they followed as well.

> If you don't have structured systems in place to capture, prioritise and resolve issues, simply asking operators for their input can be worse than not asking at all.

I didn't realise until that moment, that Sam was a leader without the title. The other operators respected Sam for his experience, expertise and his perspective. Sam was an influencer, but not in an overt, loud-mouth, extraverted, intimidating way. He was quite the opposite.

When Sam spoke with Gloria after the focus group session, Gloria was humble enough to accept that the business could've done better in the past. Sam then said, 'Tell me what help you need. I'll make sure that we [operators] do our part.'

For operators, it is harder when equipment is running sub-optimally: there's generally more work to be done, whether removing jam-ups, adjusting set up, dealing with defects and so on. So, they honestly want to help fix those issues.

Business leaders have more issues to fix than available resources. Furthermore, if they don't have structured systems in place to capture, sort, prioritise and resolve issues, simply asking operators for their input can be worse than not asking at all. Operators get tired of reported issues not being fixed. That's when they switch off.

So, while business leaders think that operators aren't interested or willing to be engaged and improve, operators know that the issue is not with them, it's with the business leaders and the improvement process. So, in their heads, they think 'it's not me, it's you who has to change'.

If I must pick one tactic from the UNLOCK Method, it is this concept that has proven to be the key issue in most places. In a recent assignment with a client, at the kick-off meeting with a nightshift team, I was there with the project lead. After the first five minutes of introductions and explanation of what the project was about, the project lead asked if the team had any questions. The very first question a frustrated operator asked was, 'Are you actually going to f###ing do something about this issue, this time?' And then, turning towards me, he continued, 'We told them what the exact issues are three years ago, and we even collected data to show the jam-up points. Nothing happened afterwards!'

So, when starting a change or an improvement journey, be ready to accept issues from the past. This is why, when picking your project leads, it is important that you pick individuals who are coachable. Why? Because they are honest and humble. These are the best leadership attributes to defuse tense moments and move things forward.

After a few more weeks in South Africa, not only did we manage to engage people like Sam, we also improved the performance and the culture of that line beyond anyone's wildest expectations. That line continued to be the star performer for that site. Mike Allen now faced the exec meetings with a spring in his step as sales were scrambling to develop sales growth plans – something they hadn't done for a few years.

This approach of getting employee input to improve processes can have an enormous impact on employees, consumers and businesses owners. This is best demonstrated through the next case study.

The Entrepreneurial Itch

Three university friends, Richard Reed, Adam Balon and Jon Wright, decided to do an experiment to scratch their entrepreneurial itch. In 1998, a few years after graduating from Cambridge, the trio started to sell smoothies from a stall at a London musical festival.

They posted a signboard on top of the stall that read, 'Should we give up our jobs to make these smoothies?' and people were asked to vote by throwing their empties into two clearly marked bin: one said 'Yes' and the other 'No'. The decision was obvious. So, nine gruelling months later (similar to the genesis of many start-ups), Innocent Drinks was born.

With a humble annual turnover of £400,000 in 1999, the company grew exponentially on the back of health-conscious UK shoppers who preferred smoothies to fizzy drinks. Sales for crushed fruit drinks rose 523% from 2001 to 2006. All through Innocent's rapid growth, they maintained their core philosophy: produce healthy, natural food and drinks that contribute to people's well-being. Along with this they took particular interest in keeping their employees engaged. This included making sure their innovation and improvement was employee-led. They reaped substantial rewards using this strategy.

One example is Claire, a seconded Bain & Co consultant, who was tasked with identifying the 'next big thing' for Innocent. With a keen eye for innovation and an understanding of market trends, Claire proposed that Innocent could revolutionise the vegetable market, similarly to what they had achieved with fruit. This idea culminated in the creation of Veg Pots – a line of ready-to-eat vegetable meals. The launch of Veg Pots marked a significant milestone for Innocent, turning into a retail phenomenon worth £30 million. This initiative didn't just expand Innocent's product line; it reinforced the importance of fresh ideas and cross-functional collaboration in driving business growth.

> Post-implementation, fulfillment rates soared from 97.5% to over 99%, and wastage plummeted to a mere 0.2% from the previous 2–3%.

Another profound contribution came from Giles, an employee from the production line. Giles observed the inefficiencies in the company's planning and forecasting processes, where each department – finance, commercial, supply chain – operated in silos with their individual reports. He proposed a unified approach, consolidating these into a singular, coherent process. This system revolutionised Innocent's operational efficiency. Post-implementation, fulfillment rates soared from 97.5% to over 99%, and wastage plummeted to a mere 0.2% from the previous 2–3%. Giles's insight not only streamlined operations, but also helped significantly to cut costs and enhance the company's environmental credentials.

This concept of leveraging ideas from new employees is well captured by movie director Nancy Meyers, in her 2015 movie *The Intern,* starring Robert De Niro. *The Intern* introduces us to Ben Whittaker (played by De Niro), a senior intern at a dynamic tech start-up. His story exemplifies the often-overlooked wisdom of age. As he immerses himself in the bustling world of online commerce, Ben's insights, drawn from decades of experience, breathe new life into the company.

For instance, he encourages the team to embrace face-to-face communication, fostering better relationships and trust among colleagues, a lesson drawn from his extensive career in traditional business. Ben's thoughtful feedback on customer service leads to improved client relations, exemplifying how his perspective benefits the company's bottom line.

His journey not only highlights the value of intergenerational collaboration, but also emphasises the need for organisations to harness the vast pool of untapped wisdom within their workforce. By providing a platform for employees of all ages, departments and seniority to share their unique insights, companies can create a culture of innovation and growth.

Innocent Drink's approach to employee engagement and empowerment is a blueprint for organisations aspiring to foster a culture of innovation and improvement. By embracing ideas from all levels of the company, Innocent not only cultivated a diverse range of products, but also nurtured a sense of ownership and pride among its employees. This inclusive culture has led to a highly motivated workforce, deeply invested in the company's success.

Innocent actively engages employees through transparent, inclusive practices and a culture that embraces learning. Monthly finance meetings led by founders promote transparency and employee involvement, fostering an understanding of the business beyond individual roles. Emphasising a supportive environment, the company encourages trying new things and views failure as a learning opportunity, with management sharing their own mistakes to reinforce unity. The open-plan office with random seating assignments enhances cross-functional interaction and holistic understanding of the company. Regular surveys assess employee motivation and satisfaction, guiding management to address concerns and maintain a positive, motivated workforce.

From these two case studies, both my personal one and Innocent Drinks, the lessons are clear: Encourage creativity, facilitate cross-functional collaboration, and most importantly, listen to your employees. The insights of employees, who are doing the tasks day in day out, can be transformative, leading to increased profitability.

And what could this success lead to? Going back to Innocent Drinks, they continued their exponential growth trajectory. In 2006, sales increased 140%, netting them £96 million. In 2007, sales reached £113.6 million delivering a 30% profit.

In 2009, Coca-Cola bought an 18% stake in Innocent for £30 million and then, in the following year, increased its shareholding to 58% for a further reported £65 million. They then increased their shareholding to over 90% for an undisclosed sum and the founders have retained a small stake with advisory roles.

Although leaders yearn for employee involvement and innovative ideas, there's a reason why operators like Sam don't speak up – they don't feel safe to bring up issues, especially if they challenge sacred cows or key individuals. So, how do you deal with those scenarios? This is what we are going to look at in the next chapter.

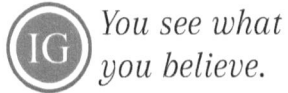

You see what you believe.

CHAPTER 5

Give it a Go

'Vulnerability is the birthplace of innovation, creativity, and change.'

– Brené Brown

They say that our best ideas come when we are in the shower. While I haven't experienced epiphanies in the shower, my most insightful thoughts have occurred during moments of tranquillity, such as reading a book, going for a walk and even waiting to pick up my sons at the train station. This inner voice seems to be quite potent and useful when it is in relaxed and protected environments, when it's feeling safe to try and fail without consequences. That's when you're most likely to give it a go. However, most workplaces do not have cultures where operators are encouraged to have a crack.

It was just such a scenario that helped me to solve one of the biggest machine downtime issues back in 2007 when I was at Arnott's Biscuits. Arnott's Shapes is a category-leading brand in the cracker biscuits aisle in Australian supermarkets, with a variety of classic flavours such as BBQ, Pizza, Cheese and Bacon, Chicken Crimpy and Cheddar, plus regular limited-edition flavours.

Most of these products got manufactured at the then-flagship site in Sydney. Commercial biscuit-making is not that different to how one would make biscuits at home – mix the dough, roll the dough sheet, cut the biscuits into shape and then bake – voilà. Factories just have bigger industrial automated machines doing it in larger continuous volumes. Around mid-2007, the

Shapes line started having some unusual jam-ups with the dough sticking to some rollers.

These automated high-speed manufacturing lines are impressive when functioning smoothly, but can quickly turn into a logistical nightmare when issues arise, akin to a major highway pile-up. Usually, the line needs to be shut down for lengthy periods to be cleaned-up before restarting. And, unfortunately, stopping these lines is like trying to turn the *Titanic*.

The manufacturing manager at the time reached out to me to see if I could help, as I was leading the site's continuous improvement program roll-out at the time. I got one of the graduate engineers to lead the project under my guidance and set up a cross-functional team with appropriate skills.

After initial scoping and set-up was completed, the project team started to gather information like Chief Detective Horatio Caine (played by David Caruso) does as soon as he arrives at a crime scene in the popular TV series *CSI: Miami*. One of those tasks is to talk to everyone who may have witnessed the crime. In our case, while it was not a crime and no one was a suspect, we spoke to all the operators across all shifts to gather information.

Most operators suggested that a recently introduced new product could be the cause. They all claimed that before this product was introduced, they didn't experience this issue. Near the end of one of the meetings, a night-shift operator mentioned that the line had gone through some major scheduled maintenance activities recently. The team took note of this information and then performed a structured root-cause analysis process to confirm if it was a contributing factor or not.

The data showed a very clear correlation between the introduction of the new product and the jam-ups. However, we know that correlation doesn't necessarily mean causation. Another handy tip when solving problems is to keep in mind that absence of evidence is not evidence of absence.

We got the process engineer to follow-up on the maintenance activities that were completed. He came to the team meeting the following week and confirmed that there had been some work carried out with the rollers. He had requested details of the tasks completed from the maintenance department.

> Another handy tip when solving problems is to keep in mind that absence of evidence is not evidence of absence.

While a few team members continued to work with the product development team to understand the scientific behavioural properties of the new product on stainless steel rollers at various temperatures, the process engineer worked with the maintenance team.

Another week later, we seemed to have irrefutable evidence of the exact root-cause – an incorrectly sized replacement cog (gear) had been mistakenly installed during the maintenance activities. All the rollers are driven with cogs attached to their central shaft, which, in turn, are connected to a motor via a chain drive. The size of the gear, based on the number of teeth, determines the speed of the roller.

If you're familiar with how the gears work on a bicycle, you will know that the chain, powered by the main cog that's attached to the pedal, will shift to a series of cogs in varying sizes, based on the gear that is been selected by the rider. The smaller the cog at the wheel end, the faster the speed. The final gauge rollers on the Shapes line each had a cog to drive the two rollers independently. However, the bottom roller had a minutely smaller cog, with just two fewer teeth, so that it would turn this roller slightly faster than the top roller. The benefit of this is it created a slight pulling effect of the dough sheet on to the web that travelled in between the rollers. However, the difference between the two cogs when placed side-by-side was not noticeable at all.

As part of the maintenance work during the recent shutdown, all the rollers were overhauled. The maintenance team had ordered two pairs of the cogs from the supplier so that the extra pair could be kept as a spare. However, the maintenance technician had picked up two of the same-sized cogs and fitted them to the rollers. This altered the speeds of the rollers and that was enough for the dough to behave in undesired ways. The issue was rectified, the maintenance records updated, and the problem disappeared.

This issue could have easily been missed if that one operator on night shift, going against everyone else who was certain that it was the new product, didn't have the courage to raise this point. Many of these hunches, gut feelings and intuitions can prove to be quite useful.

We need to create the right environment where individuals feel safe to voice their opinions and raise concerns. Rather than being risk averse, we need to create an environment where we allow individuals to try different approaches and fail safely. Such environments are conducive for process improvement. If you create the right environment for individuals to fail safely, you may be surprised by potential it can unlock.

Google vs Overture Co

In the early 2000s, Google's remarkable rise in the digital advertising space, particularly with its AdWords platform, was a pivotal moment in tech history. This success is closely tied to the culture created by co-founder Larry Page and the innovative work of key individuals like Jeff Dean (a search engineer).

In the late 1990s and early 2000s, Overture Co was the undisputed leader in search advertising. However, Larry Page, with his vision for a more equitable and open workplace, set the stage for a different kind of organisational culture at Google. This culture, characterised by safety, equality and freedom for creative problem-solving, was instrumental in attracting and retaining brilliant minds like Jeff Dean.

Google's environment, under Page's leadership, was marked by an emphasis on employee autonomy, open communication and a flat hierarchy. The staff would play outdoor games to build better teams, and there were open communication sessions where everyone was allowed to challenge decisions being made by the company without the fear of being reprimanded. This culture, along with allowing employees to experiment and innovate without the fear of failure, would set Google apart from its competitors to create the mega company we know today.

Overture's pay-per-click model was revolutionary in the late 90s, but Google's approach to advertising was different. They wanted to focus on relevancy rather than just the highest bidder. This shift was not just a technical challenge, it required a cultural one – a move towards a more user-centric advertising model. However, the bigger issue for Google was its technical capabilities to deliver that result.

In early 2002, Larry Page was deeply dissatisfied with Google's search performance. When a search is performed, there are two types of results returned: free (organic) results and the paid adverts, driven by AdWords. While the system would bring up the appropriate organic websites, the adverts it brought up were totally irrelevant.

For example, searching for 'Kawasaki H1B' would display adverts for lawyers helping immigrants with H-1B visas in the US. Larry was so frustrated with the performance of Google's ads that he printed the adverts and pinned them on the company noticeboard in the kitchen one Friday afternoon. He wrote 'THESE ADS SUCK' in big letters. That's it. He didn't send any emails, didn't schedule an emergency meeting for the following week, didn't call anyone. Instead, he just signed off for the week and went home.

Jeff Dean was hanging around in the office and when he came to the kitchen, noticed his boss' note. He, along with some of his coding colleagues, started looking at it from a different perspective. Over the weekend the team worked on a solution.

At 5:05am on Monday morning, Jeff sent out an email providing a solution to improve the accuracy of the adverts. This fix was foundational in overtaking Overture, the industry number one at the time, and building a multibillion-dollar business.

What's interesting is that Jeff and his colleagues weren't even on the team that was working on the AdWords project. No one had asked them to fix it. No one re-prioritised their work. Instead, Jeff and the colleagues took it upon themselves to provide a solution as they knew the importance of this to the company, thanks to its open communication channels. They also felt encouraged to work on it, even when it wasn't their responsibility, due to the culture that Page had created – problems were seen not as obstacles, but as opportunities. Everyone was encouraged to give it a go and, if you failed, you weren't penalised or blamed.

The improvements in AdWords with this fix were dramatic. Google's system became more efficient and effective, attracting more advertisers and users. The company's commitment to a safe, equal and innovative culture was a key differentiator, giving it a competitive edge over Overture.

> If leaders don't share their mistakes and concerns openly, neither will employees.

To develop a learning environment where employees are relaxed and feel protected, leaders need to have two specific qualities: humility and vulnerability. If leaders don't share their mistakes and concerns openly, neither will employees. Team members won't feel safe to speak up at the time, though later they may say things like, 'I knew that would happen and but didn't mention it', or 'I knew that would be a bad idea'.

I observed one site director keeping a close leash on an improvement project being deployed. The leader would attend the weekly meetings and challenge early-stage brainstorming ideas. He would provide solutions in the of hope fast-tracking results. I had to ask the leader to stay away from weekly meetings as I could see that the operators were scared to make decisions or to try various temporary solutions. He was running the project as though they were in the army, although he denied it.

You Can't Handle the Truth

Speaking of the army, the movie *A Few Good Men*, directed by Rob Reiner in 1992, is a compelling one that highlights the challenges of speaking up against a strict military culture. With a star-studded cast including Tom Cruise, Jack Nicholson and Demi Moore, the film focuses on the trial of two US marines accused of murdering a fellow marine at Guantanamo Bay.

The film illustrates the internal struggle of military personnel torn between the duty to obey orders and the moral need to seek justice. Demi Moore's character, Lieutenant Commander Joanne Galloway, assists the navy lawyer Daniel Kaffee (played by Cruise) in facing the rigid hierarchy and discipline of the military. The movie climaxes in a tense courtroom confrontation, symbolised by Jack Nicholson's portrayal of Colonel Nathan R Jessup, whose character embodies the militant culture that discourages disagreements. The movie masterfully highlights the moral dilemmas and fear of retaliation in speaking out against entrenched military traditions and command structures. Sometimes, we can have workplaces that are not too different to that.

On the flip side, if you'd like to explore concepts of vulnerability and humility and develop a corporate culture where employees feel relaxed and safe to give it a go, then the book *Dare to Lead* by Brené Brown is a compelling guide to courageous leadership. Drawing on her extensive research on vulnerability, Brown argues that true leadership requires the bravery to be vulnerable, to listen and to engage in tough conversations. She emphasises the importance of empathy, connection and the willingness to face and learn from failures. Brown offers practical tools and strategies to help leaders foster a culture of openness and resilience, where team members feel safe to take risks, speak up and innovate.

It's a call to embrace vulnerability as a strength, not a weakness, in leadership. As was the case at Google and my personal experience at Arnott's, providing a safe environment will help you unlock the seemingly disengaged employees.

Talking about Google, there is one small issue – it has now become so predictable and reliable that we turn to Google for *everything*. Are we inclined to look for digital solutions, readily ignoring our team members? How do we figure out when to go down the artificial intelligence path and when to explore the human employee potential – the natural intelligence?

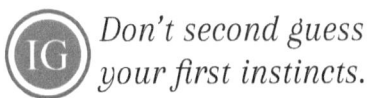

Don't second guess your first instincts.

CHAPTER 6

SMART Factories and DUMB Operators

'Train people well enough so they can leave, treat them well enough so they don't want to.'

– Richard Branson

Congrats! We are making history by going through the fourth industrial revolution at the time of writing this in early 2024. Coined as 'Industry 4.0' by the German Government in 2011 following the global financial crisis, it promises to advance the manufacturing sector with the Internet-of-Things (IoT). The so-called SMART factories, where everything within them can connect to the internet and with each other, will deliver the capability to make real-time decisions, leveraging vast amounts of current and historic data (big data). So, how did we get here? If this is the fourth revolution, when did the other three happen?

The first revolution occurred during the late 18th century, when we discovered the power of steam. This was utilised to mechanise the weaving mills, driving productivity up and costs down. Then in the early 20th century, we discovered the power of electricity. The mass assembly concept was born with electric motors powering assembly lines, again driving productivity up and costs down. You'd be familiar with Henry Ford's model T factories. By this stage, we've successfully taken people off farms and given them 'dumbed down' mundane tasks – such as tighten bolts on the left wheel as it travels along the assembly line – to repeat for an entire eight-hour work shift.

In 1939, Hewlett-Packard was registered, followed some 30 years later by Intel in 1968. Together they would go on to change the world through the power of computing, which, coupled with electric motors from the previous revolution, opened opportunities into robotics and automation. This increased speed, accuracy and repeatability, all of which improves quality and consistency, further driving productivity up and costs down.

Now, as the world is exponentially discovering the power of internet connectivity, cloud applications and networks, the promise is that we'll continue to drive productivity up and costs down. The World Economic Forum believes that this could progress to the level of implanting chips into our brains and *we* become connected to the cloud – a bit like Keanu Reeves in the movie *The Matrix* learning martial arts by inserting a kung fu chip into his brain. Artificial intelligence has made leaps and bounds in progress to make it into our everyday conversations. Despite all this, I think we're dumbing down humanity.

> Artificial intelligence has made leaps and bounds in progress to make it into our everyday conversations. Despite all this, I think we're dumbing down humanity.

Now, before we go any further, let me make it clear that I'm not anti-technology. I was in the first batch of Mechatronics Engineering graduates at the University of New South Wales in 1998, studying robotics, automation and mechanical engineering. I am for technology and technological advances. I only have two issues with technology: 1) businesses seeking technology as a silver bullet to cover for inadequate fundamental processes, and 2) businesses failing to develop the capability to understand and utilise technology to their advantage. 'Give me an example', I hear you ask. I'll provide one that covers both points.

It is common for manufacturing businesses to implement technological solutions to track machine efficiencies, machine stops, throughput rates, breakdown reasons etc. – the manufacturing 101 stuff. However, when I ask team leaders or operators the simple question, 'Are you winning or losing right now?' many cannot answer. Reason? As much as you may find it hard to believe, the issue is a lack of proper targets. When I ask operational leaders for their top three performing products, the worst downtime products, the worst waste generating products, I get blank looks. Reason? Systems aren't configured to analyse the business that way. When I request data to help teams solve problems and improve productivity, I get told that the data are not accurate, the system doesn't provide the level of detail needed,

> There are many impressive system-generated dashboards that teams are happy to flash during project meetings, even though they don't have a clue how to interpret what's in front of them!

operators don't use the correct reason codes or are unable to download the data in a useful manner for further analysis. Yet, there are many impressive system-generated dashboards that the teams are happy to flash during project meetings, even though they don't have a clue how to interpret what's in front of them! However, businesses are happy to present at major public conferences on how they are advancing with Industry 4.0! Breathe in, breathe out and relax.

Feeling Valued and Adding Value

Julian is a forklift driver and has been loading and unloading trucks for 15 years at the same site of a well-known large logistics business in Australia. Rain, hail or shine, he does this in the yard as efficiently as he can. When I worked with this site to embed a continuous improvement framework, Julian was involved in the first round of projects deployed as it involved analysing how the raw material was loaded to the line.

Julian enjoyed working on this project and made significant contributions to improving the productivity of that line by 30% within a 10-week period. Given his friendly, helpful and inquisitive nature, he was asked to participate in the next round of projects as well. Following that, it was time for Julian to step up. I recommended that we train Julian to lead a project and enrolled him in a two-day course that I was running on leading problem-solving.

I'd been watching Julian's progress over the months and thought he had potential to move into a supervisory role. During a tea break, I asked Julian if he'd be interested in progressing to a supervisory role. I mentioned that I thought he had more capacity to be harnessed. Julian thanked me for my kind words and observations. He then said, 'Ishan, although this is my full-time job, I treat this like my second job because of what I do. I don't need to think too much here, other than to watch out for safety risks. I have a side hustle that really interests me. It's like a hobby now but hopefully will turn into something bigger one day.'

I replied that he's got a great analytical mind from what I'd seen and asked why he agreed to attend the training if he wanted to just lie low. Julian said, 'Over the

> In a world where technology is improving at an exponential rate, many think that we can replace humans with automation and software.

years, we weren't given opportunities to be part of improvement projects. Mainly the engineers and the people in the office did those. We just did the work in the factory. However, with the work I've been doing with you, by being part of problem-solving teams, I feel valued and feel like I'm adding value. I'd like to lead a project. That's why I agreed to do the training.' WOW!

In a world where technology is improving at an exponential rate, many think that we can replace humans with automation and software – think about self-checkouts at supermarkets, libraries, banking, car parks, immigration and customs at airports, QR codes for ordering foods at restaurants etc.

With the fourth industrial revolution, similar to the previous ones, we are pursuing increased productivity through technology and automation. We believe labour costs are expensive, at least in first-world countries. However, we don't see the value our staff could deliver to unlock latent capacity and profitability if their potential was harnessed in the correct way. However, this issue didn't start with Industry 4.0. In fact, it had already started during the third industrial revolution, when computing was making its way into workplaces.

It's not Rocket Science or Is it?

Born in 1910 in Kansas City, Missouri, Dorothy Vaughan, an African American woman, showed early signs of mathematical brilliance, which led her to receive a full scholarship to Wilberforce University, where she graduated with a BA in mathematics at the age of 19. She continued with her passion, starting her career as a mathematics teacher.

However, her path took a significant turn in 1943 during World War II. With a shortage of men in the workforce during this time and the United States' belief that the war was going to be won in the air, President Roosevelt signed two executive orders. These would bring the defence industry together to alleviate racial, religious and ethnic discrimination.

This opened the path for Dorothy to join the National Advisory Committee for Aeronautics (NACA), something that was previously only available to White Anglo-Saxon men. However, the African Americans and White Americans would not work side-by-side, so Dorothy was assigned to the West Area Computers of the Langley Research Centre, where a segregated group of African American women made complex mathematical calculations manually using simple slide rules and graph paper. Their work involved calculating wind-tunnel and flight data, key parameters to analyse the flight characteristics of aircraft.

Dorothy's role in this group, which was also known as 'the human computers', was transformative. In 1949, she became the acting supervisor of the West Area Computers, marking her as the first African American woman to supervise staff at the centre.

A few significant events unfolded in the latter half of the 1950s that changed Dorothy's trajectory and contribution at NACA. On 4 October 1957, the Soviet Union launched Sputnik, the first satellite to be launched into an elliptical low Earth orbit, marking a major episode in the history of the Cold War. Then, on 1 October 1958, after more than 40 years of research on advancing flight, NACA would be transformed into the National Aeronautics and Space Administration (NASA), with the added responsibilities of pursuing spaceflight. Finally, IBM announced the launch of IBM7090 series computers, one of IBM's first transistor-based computers, and NASA signed up with IBM.

As their projects got larger, more complicated and riskier with space missions, NASA needed to increase the speed and improve accuracy of its calculations, and IBMs 7090 series seemed like the right strategic move. Except, there were only a limited number of people who were proficient in computer programming languages such as FORTRAN and COBOL. The IBM 7090 computers, which were larger than an average room, and required operators and technicians who knew FORTRAN.

> Recognising the imminent replacement of human computers by electronic ones, and seeing the opportunity at the same time, Dorothy proactively taught herself FORTRAN.

Recognising the imminent replacement of human computers by electronic ones, and seeing the opportunity at the same time, Dorothy proactively taught herself FORTRAN. Not only did she teach herself, but she also understood the importance of her entire team adapting to this technological shift. So, she ran unofficial after-hours classes to share her newfound knowledge with her staff, equipping them with skills that were critical in the new era of computing at NASA. This move was instrumental in transitioning her team from manual calculations to programming, thereby securing their roles in the rapidly evolving field of space exploration.

Dorothy Vaughan's story, along with two other African American women, Katherine Johnson and Mary Jackson, who made similar significant contributions to NASA, was captured by Margot Lee Shetterly in her 2016 book *Hidden Figures: The American Dream and the Untold Story of the Black Women Mathematicians Who Helped Win the Space Race*. It also got released as a movie titled *Hidden Figures,* directed by Theodore Melfi, in which there are a few notable heart-warming scenes.

In a scene after the computers are installed, Dorothy is in the main control room by herself, loading up the punched program cards, as one did back in the day. When a couple of engineers see Dorothy, one questions what she's doing in the room and implies that it is a complicated machine, just as the second engineer notices that the machine is producing the results that they'd been struggling to deliver.

As news of Dorothy's talents spreads, she is offered a temporary reassignment to the IBM team. She asks what would happen to her 'human computers' team at the West Area Computers. Upon hearing that the team would be dissolved soon, Dorothy rejects her appointment stating that she would need her team to help her program the IBM computers. In another scene, she's told that NASA is looking for a permanent IBM team. Dorothy states that her team is ready to tackle the challenge.

In a 1994 interview, Dorothy reflected on her experiences at Langley, saying, 'I changed what I could, and what I couldn't, I endured'. These words encapsulate the spirit of a woman who navigated and influenced monumental shifts in technology and society, leaving a legacy of resilience, adaptability and leadership in the face of adversity.

> 'I changed what I could, and what I couldn't, I endured.'

Being Smart about SMART Technology

In exploring how we easily dismiss human ingenuity due to various factors, such as technology, social segregation, elite backgrounds or education levels, I'm fondly reminded of the classic movie *Good Will Hunting*, directed by Gus Van Sant (1998). We see Will Hunting (played by Matt Damon), a janitor at MIT with an extraordinary mathematical talent, initially dismissed as a mere custodian, and his brilliance goes unnoticed by the academic elite. Will's hidden genius, eventually

> With all the Industry 4.0 tech solutions, yes, we are able to develop SMART factories, but at the same time, we are creating DUMB operators as well.

discovered by a professor, serves as a powerful reminder of the untapped reservoir of talent and potential that exists within organisations.

In the world today, we're surrounded by technology, even when we don't need it or haven't asked for it. For example, VW, Germany's 'everyman's' car brand, went way too far by creating full digital touchscreen dashboards and controls, which has created unprecedent customer complaints. CEO Thomas Schäfer later announced that the automaker will reintroduce physical buttons back into all VW models.

With all the Industry 4.0 tech solutions, yes, we are able to develop SMART factories, but at the same time, we are creating DUMB operators as well – operators who are constantly **D**evalued, **U**nderestimated, **M**isunderstood and **B**elittled. Sadly, they are waiting to be **D**eveloped, **U**tilised, **M**otivated and **B**elieved-in.

Technology has a place and, like everything else we've created, we need to leverage it correctly at the right place and right time. The present sad reality is that we've become slaves to technology, and it is driving us! If we think artificial intelligence is better than natural intelligence, then the end is near.

Try to avoid falling into this trap. Foster an inclusive environment that encourages all employees to contribute and collaborate with technology. By doing so, you can unlock the full potential of their workforce and, in turn, achieve extraordinary results.

However, not everyone may be wanting to collaborate. Sometimes, you need to play a game of chess to get the right people on board. How do you figure out who you need to get involved, particularly, during the early stages of your change journey?

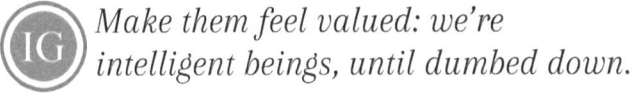 *Make them feel valued: we're intelligent beings, until dumbed down.*

CHAPTER 7

Start with Who

'Leadership is not about being in charge. It is about taking care of those in your charge.'

– Simon Sinek

I think there are two types of people in this world: those who enjoy a Krispy Kreme doughnut and those who are mindful of their diets and struggle not to eat one if placed in front of them! Okay, there may be a small third group of people who have immense will power to resist. The Australian Krispy Kreme business had been growing by double digits over a good number of years, which was causing pressure for the then chief operating officer (recently promoted at the time of writing to CEO), Nicola Steele, to keep up with the supply, as most businesses would with continual rapid growth.

Business growth is a double-edged sword. Unless you have the fundamental systems and processes in place to simultaneously run the business and improve the business (in other words, manage the daily chaos effectively and lead it to a better tomorrow), your complexity within the business will grow faster than the top line. The result? A declining bottom-line performance – net profitability as a percentage. Many business owners and general managers share with me that their businesses have grown over the last couple of years and, even with extra hours in the office, the take home profitability (as a percentage) has shrunk over that same period of time!

Krispy Kreme had some of the fundamentals in place, but they had found themselves in a tight spot with their newly launched product lines with one of their biggest customers: 7-Eleven. For overseas readers who may not be familiar with 7-Eleven, they are a global convenience store chain, known for their 24-hour service, and offering a variety of products and services, most commonly associated with fuel stations.

A significant part of Krispy Kreme's growth had come through offering 7-Eleven stores a great level of flexibility to mix-and-match the doughnut types and quantities for each store. With 13 product types, three packaging sizes, and varying quantities delivered daily in multiple truck runs to 50 stores, the packaging team needed to have their processes running like a well-oiled Swiss watch.

Unfortunately, with the unprecedent continual growth over a number of years, their processes were buckling. It was taking a team of six employees eight to 10 hours to pack all the different drops into the separate truck runs. And the biggest issue was that the drivers were running out of time to deliver to all stores and were operating on costly overtime rates.

I was asked to assist in getting a continuous improvement culture started and this was one of the processes that was keeping many people up at night. So, in trying to 'build momentum', we focused on the picking and packing processes for 7-Eleven customers at their

Sydney site first. As per the UNLOCK Method, we found our initial leader who had trust and belief in continuous improvement, picked an issue that people were passionate about, got the right mix of people into the project team and made a start. We were starting to gain decent traction when the project team hit a stumbling block when trying to implement some of process changes – resistance! Why didn't we see this coming?

Over the last decade, Simon Sinek's book and his TED talk, 'Start with "Why"', has provided great inspiration to the business world, not only to explore the 'purpose' of organisations, but also as a methodology to effectively inspire fellow employees. Sinek's 'golden circles' framework has gained immense popularity due to its simplicity, pragmatism and practicality. If you haven't seen his TED talk, I highly recommend it. You won't regret it.

Going back to our Krispy Kreme issue, I realised that we needed to start with the *who* before the *why*. We needed to think about *who* we were tapping on the shoulder to be part of our initial initiatives first, before trying to inspire the group with the *why*.

In the packing team on the factory floor was young Brian, who is headstrong and the leader without the title for this group. Brian was not quite 'actively disengaged', but close enough. Brian was not invited into the team because he was a casual who didn't work every day, and to be honest, the team hadn't expected him to be as strongly opinionated about the change. Now he was digging his heels in. The project was about halfway through and was struggling to make further significant progress. 'What do we do now?' the project lead asked me during a regular one-on-one coffee chat.

We decided to do three things: 1) have a one-on-one meeting with Brian, 2) bring Brian into the project team immediately, and 3) have focus group sessions with all the other casual staff involved with packing. During the one-on-one, Brian was pleasantly surprised that we were honestly interested in what he had to say (wasn't the first time I've experienced this and certainly won't be the last). He presented himself as a well-spoken, assertive but very cooperative individual. Not quite what we expected. The project lead welcomed him to the team and asked him to be at the next project meeting.

Then, during project meeting, the most unexpected thing happened. One of the agenda topics for that meeting was 'slow progress'. The lead was a master at asking open questions. He just asked the team, with newly added Brian at the table, 'What's the reason we can't make faster progress with these actions? Most of them are quite straight forward.' One of the team members said something along the lines of people not liking change, and they resist it.

To our surprise, Brian spoke. He said, 'There are two people who don't want to change, Mary and Chung. They are the ones you need to work on.' The project lead, without batting an eyelid, asked, 'Can you help Brian? I'm happy to help and speak with Mary and Chung.' Brian didn't need help and, surprisingly, turned out to be a great team player!

> Brian, the one we were worried about, turned out to be a great asset.

In the next couple of weeks, the team made rapid progress. Brian, the one we were worried about, turned out to be a great asset. He didn't know that it was him that the team was initially worried about, and he was instrumental in delivering a great result.

At the end, the team consistently packed all orders in about six hours with the same number of operators. And they felt like they were working less and, consequently, feeling less tired.

A few months ago, I dropped by when I was in the area. They were continuing with the same process with some further refinements. The team greeted me with smiles and waves. As I was leaving, the friendly staff handed me a couple of boxes of freshly baked doughnuts – they always do. What's my favourite? The original glaze doughnut, especially the fresh ones straight off the production line – yum!

This highlights the importance of starting with *who* first – who are the stakeholders that you need to be mindful of? Not only at the beginning of a project, but continually, especially if you hit a stumbling block like in the Krispy Kreme case. The easiest way to deal with teams and individuals who resist is to involve them, make them part of the team.

> Sometimes, if you can't completely win them over to be supportive, it is just as helpful to neutralise them – make them less resistant.

Sometimes, if you can't completely win them over to be supportive, it is just as helpful to neutralise them – make them less resistant. I've found this this is a great win-win with extremely tough, hard-core individuals who are stuck in their old ways. Generally, union leaders and their close allies behave like this; I've experienced such individuals who just resist for the sake of resisting. These are the 'actively disengaged' people. If you're project is dependent on these types of individuals, then focus on moving them to the 'disengaged' category. Better to have them being quiet, rather than bad mouthing your efforts.

The Lion King vs Pocahontas

In the captivating world of Disney's animation projects, the journey of *The Lion King* stands out as a remarkable story of transformation, not only from a technological standpoint but also in redefining Disney's future in animation movies. *The Lion King's* road to box office success wasn't as smooth as 'Hakuna Matata' (a song in the movie that means 'no worries'). In fact, it involved a twist that a few anticipated — the initial scepticism of Jeffrey Katzenberg, head of Disney's animation.

Katzenberg's career first started in the mail room at Paramount Pictures and he worked his way up through the ranks to become the head of production for motion pictures and television. When his colleague and boss at Paramount, Michael Eisner, joined Disney in 1984, Katzenberg followed.

Over the next decade, the pair would turn Disney from a struggling $2 billion company into a $22 billion empire. Katzenberg, among other accountabilities, had a special responsibility for Disney's animation division. With eagle eyes on cost-cutting, he expanded studio revenues from $320 million to $3.7 billion and pre-tax profits from $2 million to $800 million.

Much of this success was fuelled by the highly profitable animation features *The Little Mermaid* (1989), *Beauty and the Beast* (1991) and *Aladdin* (1992). Disney then wanted to accelerate, and it set a new ambitious target of one animated film per year. Therefore, after *Aladdin*, they were producing two movies simultaneously: *The Lion King* and *Pocahontas*.

The Lion King, with its African savannah backdrop and an unforgettable cast of characters, had the potential to either be a roaring success or a misguided venture into uncharted territory. Initially, Katzenberg had doubts about the viability of *The Lion King* as a major contender. Perhaps it was due to the unconventional setting or the perceived risk of deviating from the so-far-proven fairytale formula. It was considered a secondary project and lacked the full backing and resources that were typically required for Disney's flagship animations.

In a media interview, Tom Bancroft (the one who animated young Simba) stated, 'To make matters worse, at an animation staff update meeting for both films (about mid-way through *Lion King)*, Jeffery

Katzenberg told the crowd that *Pocahontas* was a "home run" while *Lion King* would be a "base hit".' Katzenberg, with his fiery, tightly controlled, no mincing of words leadership style, made it clear to everyone where he stood.

However, as time went on Katzenberg's perspective changed. Many believe the turning point was a combination of early storyboarding, character development and the recording of the timeless 'Circle of Life' song. As these elements took shape, Katzenberg started to see the potential for *The Lion King*, which transformed him from a sceptic to a champion. So, he energised the team and allocated more resources to the project.

As the animation team brought Simba, Mufasa and Scar to life, Katzenberg's leadership played a pivotal role in shaping the film's trajectory. His insights now fuelled creative discussions, leading to impactful decisions that would distinguish *The Lion King* from its predecessors. Under his guidance, the team navigated creative challenges and logistical hurdles, demonstrating resilience and adaptability.

The Lion King, therefore, evolved from a risky undertaking to a strategic masterpiece. The team's commitment to authenticity in depicting the African landscapes, and the depth of the storyline connected powerfully with audiences worldwide.

Upon its release in 1994, the film shattered box office expectations, earning over $968 million globally and securing its place as one of the highest-grossing animated films of all time. It also received two Academy Awards, numerous accolades and a permanent place in the hearts of audiences young and old. *The Lion King* defied conventional wisdom and triumphed.

> Continually monitor the engagement levels of stakeholders and see who you need to bring on board to deliver a successful outcome.

The transformative power of engaged and visionary leadership is evident here. The story also highlights the importance of stakeholder involvement, not just in endorsement but in active participation.

The two case studies here, Krispy Kreme and *The Lion King*, highlight the importance of *who* needs to be involved and engaged. They also demonstrate that no matter where you sit in the corporate ladder, engagement and involvement of key stakeholders is a key concept if you want your project to deliver exceptional results.

It is vitally important that the results are exceptional, as the next step in our UNLOCK Method is about expanding followers and that step is not going to be easy or successful with projects that have mediocre results. So, continually monitor the engagement levels of stakeholders and see who you need to bring on board to deliver a successful outcome.

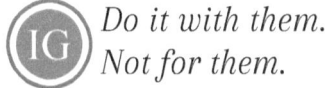
*Do it with them.
Not for them.*

CHAPTER 8

Flaws and Fortunes

'I have not failed. I've just found 10,000 ways that won't work.'

– Thomas Edison

Sometimes we can score our greatest victories in the least expected ways. In this section, we're exploring gaining traction. We need to deliver results fast and to do so, we must leverage not only our strengths but, sometimes, our weaknesses as well. We need to break through obstacles and hurdles to build success.

Shiraaz is a team leader on night shift for a large manufacturing company that I've recently worked with. Shiraaz has an extremely warm personality. He likes to keep his team on a high-energy vibe to make it easier for everyone to get through those unearthly, literally dark hours.

From my experience of working in FMCG (fast-moving consumer goods) factories, I know that night-shift teams in general have a unique vibe about them. I've often wondered if this is because they know that there's no one around to help them when things go wrong – compared with day shift teams who can call on other departments, such as engineering, quality, safety and HR if needed – so, they have this sense of comradery usually not seen across day and afternoon shifts.

I was about to attend Shiraaz's newly formatted shift start-up huddle meeting, which was standardised across all shifts. Shiraaz, with his long-beard, greeted me with his usual warm smile as we caught up over a coffee to prepare for his meeting – going through the structure and intent, and facilitating tips. As soon as we walked up to the meeting area, I noticed something different.

The team of about 30 mostly male operators in high-vis clothing were all huddled up close to the whiteboard, which contained all their shift-related information, almost like a scrum in a rugby match. I couldn't help but compare this with what I'd noticed on day and afternoon shifts in the same factory. Everyone would stand right at the back, leaning against the far wall, and it would take a lot of effort by the team leader to get them closer to the board. Even then, it wouldn't be uncommon to see a handful of individuals still hanging back. I could almost see the distribution of employees who are engaged, actively disengaged and the seemingly disengaged quiet quitters, simply by where they were standing.

> I could almost see the distribution of employees who are engaged, actively disengaged and the seemingly disengaged quiet quitters, simply by where they were standing.

I certainly felt and noticed the difference with Shiraaz's night-shift team as we walked in, with head nods and warm smiles, acknowledging the visitor – me. Shiraaz walked up to the board and started his meeting with some friendly banter, before getting to the formal agenda topics. After going through safety and quality information and discussion points, he got onto the productivity – yesterday's performance numbers. That's when I noticed something unusual.

Shiraaz asked the team, pointing to the performance metrics for each line, 'Who can see what this colour is? Is it green or red? What number did we hit yesterday?' A couple of guys who worked on that part of the factory promptly responded. He continued to move to the next line and asked the same question, 'Ok, what about this line?' Responding to a slight delay from the group, Shiraaz continued, 'Come on guys, help me. You know I'm colour blind. I can't see if we had a good day or not. How did we do yesterday on this line?'

On a side note, Shiraaz knows exactly how each line performed – he completes the shift report at the end of each shift and comes in early to update the team meeting board. I was there when he did that, however, I didn't realise that he's colour blind and he'd labelled his red and green whiteboard markers so that he knows which is which. My respect for Shiraaz amplified immensely.

Shiraaz has managed to turn a weakness to his strength. His team is aware of this situation and, given his warm personality, they just play along. The playful nature, the comradery, the support and caring for one another is what has made this team special.

I wondered if companies could do at a team or even organisational level what Shiraaz was demonstrating at an individual level.

Sticky Situation

That's when I came across how Post-It® Notes were born. These innocent little yellow pieces of paper that we've become so used to, relying on them to remind us of various tasks, were actually an accidental discovery!

In 1968, Dr. Spencer Silver, a 3M senior scientist, was trying to create a stronger adhesive for the aerospace industry when he discovered an acrylic adhesive with unique properties. It formed clear spheres and stuck lightly to surfaces but didn't bond tightly to them. At the time, 3M management doubted it had any commercial viability and it was deemed a failure in terms of the research brief Dr Silver had been given – develop an adhesive that is permanent, stronger and tougher for the aerospace industry.

Meanwhile, Arthur Fry, another 3M scientist, was

frustrated. Every Wednesday night, while practicing with his church choir, he would use little scraps of paper to mark the hymns they were going to sing in the upcoming service. By Sunday, he'd find that most of the pieces of paper had fallen out of the hymnal. He was looking for a bookmark that would stick to his hymnal without damaging it.

He was exploring potential solutions and had a Eureka moment when he remembered a presentation he had attended on Silver's unique adhesive. Working together, Silver and Fry developed a prototype sticky bookmark and found themselves writing messages to communicate around the office. That's when it hit them that there was more to their humble semi-adhesive bookmark!

Finally in 1977, nearly three years after Fry's moment of epiphany, 3M reluctantly released the product under the brand name 'Press n' Peel'. Two years later, 3M provided full support and gave the product a second go by implementing a massive free sampling campaign. Ninety per cent of businesses that received the free samples re-ordered it!

Then on 6 April 1980, Silver and Fry's accidental creation appeared in US stores as Post-It® Notes. Today, 600 Post-It® Note products are sold globally, with 3M selling more than 50 billion individual notes per year. By the way, according to 3M, its iconic canary yellow colour was also chosen accidentally – the lab next door only had yellow scrap paper available for a trial.

The Post-It® Note's journey from a perceived failure to a globally celebrated success highlights several key insights about turning flaws into fortunes. However, this is not surprising for a company like 3M, which itself was founded as a failed mine.

In 1902, the Minnesota Mining and Manufacturing Company (3M) was registered and embarked on a venture to mine corundum in Minnesota. However, they discovered their mineral deposit contained anorthosite, not corundum, derailing their initial mining plans. Despite this setback, the struggling 3M company pivoted to manufacturing abrasive products.

The company fostered a culture for innovation from the beginning. They established a '15% rule', which allowed scientists to spend 15% of their time on independent research projects – of which, clearly, the humble Post-It® Note is the poster child.

However, they have profited from pure accidents as well. In 1953, lab technicians Patsy Sherman and Joan Mullen were working on a project when Mullen accidentally dropped a beaker of the fluid on her shoes.

Observing that it was impossible to get the fluid off Mullen's shoes, Sherman later developed it further to make it a viable and valuable product. Scotchgard fabric protector is the result.

Creativity thrives through collaboration. Silver's adhesive required Fry's perspective to unlock its true potential to bring Post-It® Notes to the world. This would not have occurred if not for a culture of openness and cross-functional interaction. It demonstrates that the path from idea to application is not a solo endeavour but a collaborative exploration from different viewpoints and experiences. Hence the cross-functional problem-solving approach with the UNLOCK Method

> Creativity thrives through collaboration.

The Show Must Go On

Stories such as 3M's Post-It® Notes helps us to embrace our weaknesses, engage collaboratively and foster environments where creativity can flourish. Consequently, we can turn our vulnerabilities into our greatest strengths, both in personal growth and within the complex organisational culture.

We see this being brought to life by the very creative

Australian movie director, Michael Gracey, with the 2017 biographical musical film, *The Greatest Showman*, portraying the life of PT Barnum, a visionary showman and entrepreneur, who was not without his share of controversies.

The story begins in the early 19th century, showing Barnum's humble beginnings and his dream for a bigger life. Barnum (played by Hugh Jackman) had a talent for turning perceived weaknesses into strengths. He transforms his museum into a circus by adding unique performers who were often considered outcasts due to their distinct physical attributes or abilities. These include individuals like the bearded lady, Lettie Lutz, and performer Charles Stratton, who had dwarfism.

> When we're trying to gain traction and momentum with the UNLOCK Method, we need to use everything we've got, sometimes even our weaknesses.

In the movie, Barnum places adverts asking for people with flaws to turn up for an audition. Barnum's ability to see the extraordinary in the unconventional and his flair for showmanship turn these performers into stars, ultimately leading to the success of his circus, despite societal prejudices and criticisms.

The movie shows a somewhat romanticised Barnum navigating the complexities of life and the demands of an entrepreneur. He also shows the spirit of achieving one's dreams through grit, balancing life and business and, most importantly, the idea of turning flaws and uniqueness into advantageous positions delivering fortunes.

This is an important point to remember: when we're trying to gain traction and momentum with the UNLOCK Method, we need to use everything we've got, sometimes even our weaknesses.

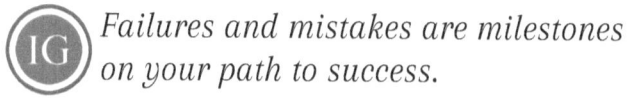 *Failures and mistakes are milestones on your path to success.*

CHAPTER 9

Adapting to Triumph

Everyone has a plan till they get punched in the face.

– Mike Tyson

When executing any plan, particularly when implementing change, one thing that we can all agree on is that the reality often turns out to be different to the plan. Consequently, we are forced to change our plans mid-flight, adapting and improvising to somehow get to the original destination.

In 2014, Kellogg was building a second factory in India to keep up with the rapid growth in demand it had been experiencing. With the old site situated in the north-western mega city of Mumbai, Kellogg strategically decided to build the new site in the south-eastern region, where a new mega industrial hub, 'Sri City', was being developed on the border of two states: Tamil Nadu and Andra Pradesh.

My first visit, along with some senior Asia Pac supply chain leaders, to Sri City revealed the challenges of such developments in remote locations, including major infrastructure being developed at the same time, companies competing to hire the extremely limited pool of builders and technicians, and few potential employees due to lack of nearby townships.

The biggest challenge, apart from getting the site built, was securing and training the operators. Kellogg India formulated a unique and a creative plan to address this. The thinking was, if we can't find them, then let's develop them!

There were two critical parts to making this happen: finding the right people and providing them with the right skills. They partnered with some of the best vocational schools and technical colleges in the region to develop a customised curriculum, specifically designed to provide the necessary skills. This included hands-on, theoretical and team behavioural modules. The six-month program was designed to take a high school graduate and provide them with the basic skills and mindset to work in a manufacturing environment. This was complemented by training at the old site in Mumbai for them to get the real experience.

The second part of the plan was finding the right people. The India Kellogg HR team went to all the local schools surrounding the Sri City area on a recruitment drive. The recruitment process focused on finding students with the right thinking, attitude and drive. This last part, the drive, was something unique. They were particularly after individuals who were driven to have a strong career path so they could help their own families. In essence, Kellogg wanted students who were committed, not only to advancing themselves, but who had a mindset of helping and advancing more than themselves. This, in turn, helps to advance the small townships these students came from, at least in a small way. Often, we hear that we should recruit for the attitude as it is easier to provide the skills. This was a classic example of that in practice.

The site leadership team and their direct reports at the new site – the extended leadership team – needed industry experience along with passion to develop a new culture at Sri City. So, they were recruited through the usual process (advertise, shortlist, interview, hire) as long as they had the right experience and the drive. Sreenivasulu Suram was one of the new recruits. He had a great track record, and he joined the maintenance team as an assistant manager.

Then, there was good news and some bad news. The good news was that the recruitment process had been progressing exceptionally well. Almost 95% of the required operators had been hired and were now going through the special skills program. The bad news was that the engineering build was going to be delayed due to all the challenges mentioned, as well as issues with equipment providers. The estimate was about a six- to eight-month delay.

> How do you keep all the freshly recruited, trained and graduated employees engaged while they are twiddling thumbs on site?

How do you keep all the freshly recruited, trained and graduated employees engaged while they are twiddling thumbs on site? There was not much more training in the fundamentals to be provided. So, the team had a major challenge in keeping the employees engaged. That's when Suram, in consultation with the site leadership team, came up with the greatest improvised activity that I've come across that adapts and rolls with the punches – so to speak.

Suram and I just happened to be speaking about engaging employees to conduct various minor maintenance activities, such as lubricating machine parts, inspecting overall machine performance and keeping the equipment in mint condition until the new site was ready. I was sharing with him some photos and concepts of internal training programs developed by one of the leading global companies based in US that I'd had the privilege of visiting. Suram was asking a lot of

> By collaborating with the various departments, such as safety, quality and HR, Suram developed an advanced curriculum that would help the site to create a high-performing culture.

questions about the modules they provided and how they delivered it.

While exploring options with the site leadership team, Suram came up with an unusual idea. He wanted to make use of the idle operators by providing them with the next level in training and team-building activities.

By collaborating with the various departments, such as safety, quality and HR, Suram developed an advanced curriculum that would help the site to create a high-performing culture. This would be fitting for the young operators, who had already gone through some out-of-the-box training at the technical colleges.

However, how could he train operators on high-level technical skills when the equipment installation was delayed? That was the brilliance of Suram's improvisation. Technically, what the operators lacked was understanding of basic maintenance principles, causes of machine failures and advanced tool-handling competence. And what is the most common mechanical machine available in any remote part of a developing country? The humble bicycle.

He went to the local market and bought a couple of bicycles that were in very bad condition. He then created a makeshift workshop in the empty warehouse area and got all the operators divided into groups.

Their challenge? Dismantle the bicycles into the smallest parts possible – literally into pieces of twisted and rusted metal parts, nuts and bolts. He got the operators to understand the basics of machine part failures as well as their functionality. All the dismantled parts were methodically and systematically laid out on the concrete floor in the empty warehouse by each working team.

The next challenge was to categorise all the parts into parts that were in good shape, could be repaired and needed replacing. Suram watched with interest how the team cleaned, washed, straightened, repaired and painted all the parts. When he was given a list of spare parts they needed, he challenged them to see if they *actually* needed everything and whether they had tried to restore any of the existing parts. The cost of spare parts they needed wasn't much, but the learning was priceless.

Soon the teams were re-assembling their restored bicycles. Finally, they were riding the bikes around the half-built factory, grinning from ear-to-ear. It was great to observe how, by using these piles of junk, it had increased the team's engagement and improved mechanical aptitude, all while contributing to a better factory start-up.

This program did wonders in not only keeping the idle

operators busy during the delayed factory start-up, but also bringing the teams closer. This was reflected in the results and the culture once the factory started up. It was also of high interest to most of the other neighbouring multi-national factories that were being built. They frequently toured this site to understand the details of the training and observe the culture it helped to create.

Streaming Success

When I was young boy, I enjoyed watching the TV programs *MacGyver* and *The A-Team*. I watched them build incredibly useful contraptions out of pieces of junk or ordinary items that were just lying around using their applied science knowledge. They used these devices to solve complicated missions and help innocent victims.

Sometimes, we can deliver great outcomes and value by using things just lying around gathering dust right under our noses, as long as we are prepared to improvise and adapt. This valuable mindset is needed to deliver rapid results. I can think of numerous situations where teams have used discarded machines, borrowed parts from another site, or got better utilisation from machines through changing configurations and so on.

Adaptability can even lead to building highly successful global companies.

In the late 1990s, colleagues Reed Hastings and Marc Randolph, both serial entrepreneurs who had already started several companies and who were early adopters of internet technology, were exploring business opportunities during their daily commute to work: a 45-minute drive each way from Santa Cruz to Sunnyvale in California.

One of the ideas they had explored was a videotape rent-by-mail service. If you're a Gen Z or younger reader, videotapes were the movie format of choice prior to DVDs. Please don't ask what a DVD is. They initially discarded the idea due to the practicalities, namely the difficulty with packaging, but after they tested mailing an old music CD to themselves, and it arrived intact, they thought the idea could work.

In 1997, they started Netflix to offer a different service to that being offered by the global giants Blockbuster and VideoEzy, which dominated the entertainment industry through physical stores at the time. Hastings and Randolph were trying to solve customer frustrations, such as the inconvenience of going to physical stores, paying late fees and the limited availability of titles. Their first website was launched on 14 April 1998 to provide a better service by adapting to those customer needs.

After surviving the dot-com crash, Netflix's transition to a subscription-based model in 1999 was a pivotal move. It addressed two main challenges: the delay in DVD delivery and the high demand for new releases. The subscription model not only improved customer retention by encouraging repeat rentals, but also diversified rental patterns through a personalised movie recommendation system.

As streaming technology advanced, Netflix once again adapted, launching its video-on-demand streaming service in 2007, making it accessible in more than 190 countries in 2016. This move, initially seen as a complementary service to DVD rentals, eventually became Netflix's core offering. The company's strategic partnerships, like with Microsoft for Xbox 360 streaming, expanded its reach and sealed its market position.

Netflix also ventured into original content production. Shows like *House of Cards* and *Orange is the New Black* marked Netflix's entry into producing its own series, distinguishing it from traditional networks.

Netflix leveraged data analytics to understand viewer preferences and behaviours. The platform uses algorithms to recommend content tailored to individual user tastes, enhancing the user experience and keeping subscribers engaged.

Netflix's approach to dealing with competition further highlights its adaptability. While Blockbuster clung to the traditional retail rental model, Netflix offered convenience and flexibility. This adaptability was key to Netflix overtaking Blockbuster in the market. But before this happened, Netflix was nearly sold to Blockbuster.

Despite its growth, Netflix posted losses in its initial years, which kept the two founders sleepless at night. In early 2000, they met with Blockbuster's then-CEO John Antioco to strike a deal. They offered to sell Netflix to Blockbuster, which was a $6 billion corporate giant at the time, for $50 million. Hastings and Randolph wanted to continue Netflix as Blockbuster's online arm under 'Blockbuster.com'. Blockbuster turned them down.

In 2002, Netflix's IPO (initial public offering) raised $82.5 million despite its early losses, highlighting its growth potential. Blockbuster struggled to adapt and eventually lost to Netflix's innovative approach. Despite having 9000 stores in its heyday, Blockbuster filed for bankruptcy in 2010.

Meanwhile Netflix, as we enter 2024, has grown to 247 million subscribers, with an estimated revenue of $33.5 billion and a market cap around $245 billion.

Throughout its evolution, Netflix's commitment to innovation, customer-centricity and strategic adaptability has been critical. From technological advancements in streaming and cloud computing to content curation and global expansion, Netflix has continually adapted to stay connected with its customers.

The lesson here is clear: success in today's dynamic environment demands agility, foresight and a relentless pursuit of adaptation. Netflix didn't just adapt to change: they anticipated it, embraced it and, in many ways, created it.

> The lesson here is clear: success in today's dynamic environment demands agility, foresight and a relentless pursuit of adaptation.

Reversing the Logic

Sometimes we're forced into situations where adaptation and improvisation become the only way to survive – literally! The 1995 movie *Apollo 13*, directed by Ron Howard, provides a captivating illustration of the transformative power of adaptability and improvisation during adverse situations.

The film is a dramatic retelling of the true story of the ill-fated *Apollo 13* mission, which suffered a catastrophic oxygen tank failure while enroute to the moon. In the face of life-threatening technical challenges and limited resources, the astronauts, along with NASA's ground control team, had to adapt swiftly and improvise solutions to ensure their safe return to Earth. They displayed remarkable resilience, creativity and a shared commitment to the mission's success.

It is a great example of how individuals and teams can deliver outstanding outcomes when confronted with adversity. It shows the importance of fostering a culture that encourages adaptability, problem-solving and effective communication.

During disastrous situations, the problem-solving is flipped from not trying to find what's broken, to trying to figure out what is working and then leveraging those processes. In my research for my previous book

ADVANCE, I interviewed retired Qantas pilot Captain Richard de Crespigny to understand his approach with the Airbus A380 mid-air engine blowout in 2010 on a routine Singapore to Sydney flight with 469 people on board. His approach was exactly the same: 'The flight cockpit lit up like a Christmas tree with error messages. We couldn't figure out the extent of the damage up in the air. We worked with what we knew was still working.'

This thinking highlights our ability to improvise and adapt under difficult conditions. With organisations, just as in space exploration and aviation, unforeseen challenges arise. To thrive in such environments and situations, it's critical to nurture teams that value adaptability and encourage employees to think on their feet – improvise.

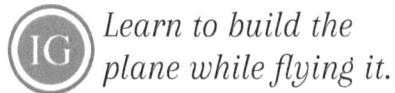
Learn to build the plane while flying it.

'It had long since come to my attention that people of accomplishment rarely sat back and let things happen to them. They went out and happened to things.'

– Leonardo da Vinci

At the turn of the decade from the 1980s to the 1990s, New York City was struggling with soaring crime rates and its subway was a symbol of decay. Graffiti covered the trains, fare evasion was significantly on the rise and the homicide rates reflected a city in crisis.

When William Bratton was appointed as the man in charge of New York City's transit police in 1990, he wanted to take a different approach to combat this issue. He looked into the broken windows theory, introduced by social scientists James Q. Wilson and George Kelling in 1982, which suggested that addressing small crimes and maintaining order in public spaces can prevent more serious crimes.

In fact, Kelling was already consulting for the Metropolitan Transportation Authority (MTA) when Bratton took charge and had already recommended the graffiti be cleaned from the train carriages; however, there was little evidence to suggest that this approach was effective yet, as it was early days.

Bratton, wanting to take this approach to the next level, implemented further measures, such as arresting turnstile jumpers. In 1991, officers were arresting around 1400 fare evaders per week, sending a message that even minor breaches of law would be prosecuted.

In 1994, Bratton was promoted to New York City

police commissioner, and he expanded his approach citywide, with a 'quality of life initiative' targeting minor offences like vandalism, public drinking and street prostitution.

By the mid-1990s, major offences on the subway system had dropped by 75%. The citywide murder rate fell from 2245 in 1990 to 633 in 1998, a decline of over 70%. There was a significant improvement in the public's perception of safety in the subway system: a 1997 survey found that 75% of subway riders felt safer than they had five years earlier.

However, the policy was not without controversy. Critics argued that it led to over-policing and racial profiling, disproportionately affecting communities of colour. A significant number of misdemeanour arrests involving Black and Hispanic New Yorkers raised concerns about racial bias in law enforcement.

By 1997, the *New York Times* reported a 9.1% drop in the city's crime rate, with murders reaching their lowest level since 1967. This trend continued into the 2000s under Mayor Michael Bloomberg, with New York City experiencing a further decline in crime rates. In Bloomberg's final year in 2013, the city had 333 murders, a significant decrease from the 2000 murders a year in the early 1990s. The broken windows approach also helped with social changes, such as the decline in the cocaine epidemic.

The success of the broken windows theory in New York influenced its adoption in other cities, although its efficacy and ethical implications continue to be debated. Malcolm Gladwell's book *The Tipping Point: How little things can make a big difference* is a great resource examining this theory.

Wildfires and Campfires

Step 3 of the UNLOCK Method, Expand Followers, is about how we can reach the tipping point of our own change journey. Author Everett M. Rogers, in his book *Diffusion of Innovations*, provides the best context to understand the tipping point.

Rogers states that for an idea to disseminate through a population, it first needs to be adopted by the subgroup he calls the 'innovators'. These are the individuals who are willing to take on risks and like to be seen as trendsetters. Rogers claims that these people make up about 2.5% of the population. Next are the 'early adopters' (13.5%), who are also quick to take up new technology, and can be enthusiastic champions.

Collectively, these two groups make up the critical mass (16%) that is needed to tip a system to generate momentum for the idea to spread like wildfire. Following that, we need to convert the 'early majority' (34%), who will not buy into an idea until the first 16% have tried it. The early majority will often seek advice from the early adopters as they are slightly risk averse. To complete Rogers' model, the fourth category is the 'late majority' (34%) and the fifth category is the 'laggards' (16%).

Expanding on Rogers' model, author Geoffrey Moore provided more detail on this concept in his book *Crossing the Chasm*. Moore claims that, for an idea to reach the tipping point, it needs to reach at least the early majority stage – that is a minimum of 16% in total have to embrace the idea.

> For an idea to reach the tipping point, it needs to reach at least the early majority stage – that is a minimum of 16% in total.

So, if you were looking for a mathematical formula, you need to get 16% of your employees to be torchbearers for your change journey to gain momentum. Until then, you need to drive the change for them, with the pedal to the metal.

Continuing with my teenage hiking trip in Sri Lanka that I shared on page 27, after the first night's successful campfire, we got the hang of it. In fact, we improved on the process by cutting and drying some of the grass on the rocks of the fire ring during the day, which we used as kindling. We took turns to collect firewood as a way of sharing the load.

During the day, we explored the area. One of the attractions within Horton Plains is a beautiful natural wonder created by a dramatic cliff with a drop around 1200 metres, aptly named 'World's End'. It offers breathtaking panoramic views of the rolling hills and lush greenery of the surrounding plains, and the tea-plantation villages in the valley way below look like miniature buildings and roads.

Starting the fire in the next few evenings felt less pressured as it was a repeat process. At the end of the week-long camp, we walked down the hill to the train station with lighter backpacks, richer friendships and amazing experiences.

So, combining my camping analogy and Rogers' diffusion of innovation theory, we're aiming to get our change journey to a tipping point by getting more of the early majority involved. And to do that, we share activities and early success news to help others embrace the idea.

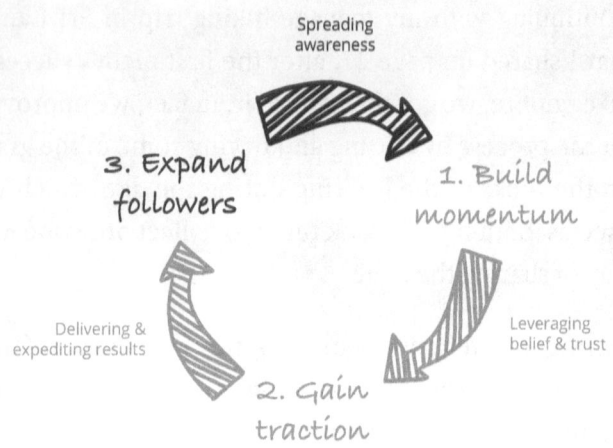

Figure 6: UNLOCK Framework Step 3 – Expand followers.

The three concepts that we will explore under this step are:

Chapter 10: Name it

Christening any project, program or initiative helps to give it life and increases ownership. Many global manufacturing companies have adopted this technique for their operational excellence programs. We learn from statesmen Nelson Mandela and Mahatma Ghandi how they used this technique to move entire nations.

Chapter 11: Leverage Their Ego

Abraham Maslow popularised his theory of the hierarchy of needs to understand motivational factors for human behaviour. The five layers of needs are physiological, safety, love and belonging, esteem, and self-actualisation. In an unusual setting, I came across how this plays an important role when we are seeking people to lead our campaign. After all, we do love to share our accomplishments with our friends in social settings. If we can provide opportunities for individuals to brag, in a humble way, then we can help them to tick off their esteem needs. How else would Ernest Shackleton convince his crew of 27 to join him on his expedition to Antarctica in 1912?

Chapter 12: Rising Tide Lifts All Boats

Playfulness, progress and persistence play a massive role in creating an infectiously positive culture. It helps to create an atmosphere that lifts people up and increases the likelihood of the fence sitters getting involved – which is exactly what we want to expand our followers. We learn from one of the pioneering online retaining companies, Zappos, in the US, how they went about leveraging employee engagement to create a positive culture.

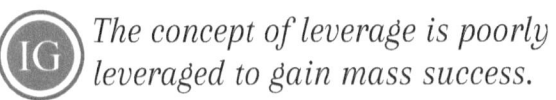

The concept of leverage is poorly leveraged to gain mass success.

CHAPTER 10

Name it

'As we develop new beliefs about who we are, our behaviour will change to support the new identity.'

– Tony Robbins

Let's play a game. Below are 10 well-known slogans used globally in advertising. Can you name the company or the product? I've removed the product names from the slogans where it was part of it – didn't want to make it too easy for you…

1. Just do it.
2. Think different.
3. Because you're worth it.
4. Have a break, have a _____.
5. The ultimate driving machine.
6. There are some things money can't buy. For everything else, there's _____.
7. Diamonds are forever.
8. _____ gives you wings.
9. Keep walking.
10. Hello Moto.

How did you go? You can check your answers at the bottom of the page.[1]

Many would agree that Nike's 'Just do it' is perhaps the most recognised slogan, so much so, that it has made it into our own business vocabulary, usually attributed

---

1 Here are the correct answers: 1) Nike, 2) Apple, 3) L'Oréal, 4) KitKat, 5) BMW, 6) MasterCard, 7) De Beers, 8) Red Bull, 9) Johnnie Walker, and 10) Motorola.

to classify quick-win initiatives that are simply no-brainers.

Then, there are also slogans created with no brains. I came across three when researching material for this chapter that I simply couldn't believe companies went ahead with. For example, Sega, the video gaming company, had 'The more you play with it, the harder it gets'. The sportswear giant Reebok seems to have had the worst slogan (in my opinion) in Germany that understandably lasted only a very short time: 'Cheat on your girlfriend, not on your workout.' Would you step into an aircraft, where the company's slogan read 'Good luck'? Uzbekistan Airways' slogan did, which was put down to a case of 'lost in translation'.

> There are two aspects from a human psychology perspective we are trying to leverage: memory and pride.

Slogans in marketing campaigns help to keep the product or the service front of mind with their customers. Companies also use Hollywood and sports stars as brand ambassadors to position products in our subconscious mind through powerful imagery.

At a basic level, there are two aspects from a human psychology perspective we are trying to leverage: memory and pride. These help us to remember the product or the service and make us feel good to be associated with it. For example, Apple users feel good and proud to be called an Apple user. I'd like to borrow this thinking for this third part of the UNLOCK Method: expanding followers by spreading awareness.

Mark, the operational excellence director for a global pharmaceutical company, was given a challenge. Leverage their legacy operational excellence framework and develop and implement a next-level program to advance the company's performance and unlock constrained capacity.

During our early conversations, I thought that Mark's timelines and milestones were extremely aggressive, but he was happy to move other variables to deliver the promised milestones.

Mark's challenge wasn't just developing a framework; he had to drive the change across all of the 25 manufacturing sites globally, both from philosophical and technical viewpoints. In both cases, the site teams needed to unlearn and relearn. Philosophically, the leadership teams needed to understand how the various parts connected; how it was different to the previous framework; how to leverage it to deliver performance at their sites and so on. Technically, all the champions needed to understand the difference in the approaches, the tools, the techniques, the steps, the sequences and so on.

And being in the healthcare industry, processes are controlled to an extremely high standard – as one would expect. Yet, in little over 15 months, Mark had delivered the program, taken it around the world, trained all the key stakeholders and made a noticeable difference to their performance metrics. How did he do it?

Having walked alongside the global team and been involved in some of their workshops, here's what I noticed.

Naming it

Right from the outset, Mark gave the program a specific name, as opposed to the generic 'operational excellence program'. The company itself had gone through a name change and a branding refresh, so he capitalised on that wave of excitement. Mark incorporated this new improved program into the overall corporate identity change.

A name change alone doesn't help if individuals can't identify it, recognise it or associate with it, and that's where the branding came in. Mark created a logo and a tagline to bring the program alive.

Week-long bootcamp training sessions were held in a few strategic locations around the world for all senior leaders and key individuals from each site.

The structure, the preparation, the detail and the content of the bootcamp had a certain vibe: this is the newly upgraded program roll-out and you don't want to miss it. Of course, having the backing and the support from the chief supply officer of the company did help. The week wasn't a death-by-PowerPoint training program, it was delivered as an intensive and immersive experience.

Taking everything to the next level, Mark and his team created a series of professionally developed animations to explain the program. The benefit of branding truly shone through these videos, which were narrated by professional voice-over artists.

When I walked into the first bootcamp in the Asia Pacific region, which was held at one of their strategic sites in southeast Asia, I was simply blown away by what I saw. There were flags with the program name by the entrance to the main building, posters by reception, we were asked to sign the commitment poster that was on an easel under a spotlight, and there were special stickers on the floor leading from reception to the training room. This was the best first impression I'd ever had for a program launch.

And then I entered the training room. Based on what I had experienced up to that point, I had naturally raised my expectations, and yet I was still blown away! Two giant screens glowing with program logos greeted me. A massive banner in between the screens and more pull-up banners across the peripheries confirmed that I was in the right room.

As I stood there absorbing the impressive set-up, I was interrupted by a friendly usher handing me a lanyard with my name on it. I was taken to the head delegate table, which was strategically placed in the front corner. I took my assigned seat with a name tag sitting on spacious, white table-clothed tables. The rest of the training room was equally impressive with white tablecloths, name tags, and even little flags on each table reminding us of the program we were rolling out.

During the entire week, the same standards were upheld – various branded gifts and souvenirs were handed out to winners of activities and quizzes, branded gift packs were given to all attendees, and a certificate of completion was delivered in a leather folder with the certificate on one side and the group photo on the other.

The feedback provided by the participants, a 4.95 rating out of 5, was fitting, unsurprising and concurs that the program launch was highly successful.

Now, I feel obliged to clarify something here. While all of this – the gifts, the branding, the souvenirs, the videos – may come across as superficial, it was anything but. I don't want you to think that driving major change initiatives or unlocking excellence can be achieved purely through surface-level branded corporate merchandise. This is the icing on the cake. Mark and his global team had conducted multiple stakeholder engagement sessions, global workshops to develop the framework, benchmarking with industry best practices to understand gaps before developing their new program. What I've shared with you here is how they deployed it in a way that made it easier for employees to embrace and embody it.

Mark's intentions were clear – anything that has the program name associated with it had to be of a very high standard. So, he unapologetically

> Don't think that unlocking excellence can be achieved purely through surface-level branded corporate merchandise. This is the icing on the cake.

developed and delivered an exceptional program for employees that had the capability to take company's global manufacturing performance to the next level.

Unfortunately, during the early program deployment stage, the company restricted international travel for the entire company – multinational companies do this from time to time to manage expenses. Upon hearing the news, several previous participants wrote directly to the chief supply officer asking them not to cancel the bootcamps because of the value they delivered and the importance of the program. The company lifted the travel ban for the program deployment, which is how I got the opportunity to be part of the subsequent bootcamps, continuing to support the global team with the deployment in the Asia Pacific region.

It's indicative of the impact this initiative had on employees that they wrote to the chief supply officer, a very senior role in the organisational hierarchy, requesting they not cancel travel for the deployment of the program. To me, it goes back to the reason

> Such is the power of naming a program – it makes it memorable and it makes individuals feel proud to be part of it, associated with it and seen using it.

why Apple users like to be seen in airport lounges with their illuminated Apple logos on the back of their laptops – they are proud to be associated with the brand.

Such is the power of naming a program – it makes it memorable and it makes individuals feel proud to be part of it, associated with it and seen using it. This approach has worked not only in organisations, but also in politics as well.

Mandela's Victory

In the early 1990s, South Africa was a nation going through monumental change. The apartheid regime's decades-long stronghold on the country was weakening and the winds of democracy were beginning to blow.

In the lead up to South Africa's first democratic elections in 1994, the African National Congress (ANC), led by Nelson Mandela, launched a pivotal campaign named 'Ready to govern'. It wasn't just a campaign slogan; it was a statement of intent, a promise and a beacon of hope for millions.

It was also a strategic communication tool that demonstrated ANC's preparedness to evolve from a liberation movement, which had fiercely battled apartheid, into a fully-fledged governing political party.

It resonated with the ANC's determination to assume the reins of political power responsibly.

Mandela, a symbol of resilience and statesmanship, was the central figure in this transformative campaign. His personal sacrifice and unwavering dedication to a united South Africa lent credibility to the ANC's vision for a future founded on the principles of democracy, justice and equality.

Mandela understood the importance of messaging to convey a sense of preparedness, responsibility and a forward-looking vision – all crucial elements in winning the trust of the nation. As Mandela led the charge, the 'Ready to govern' campaign became a rallying cry for millions of South Africans yearning for a just and democratic nation.

> Mandela understood the importance of messaging to convey a sense of preparedness, responsibility and a forward-looking vision...

On 27 April 1994, the first democratic elections in South Africa were held, removing the shackles of apartheid. Then on 9 May 1994, Mandela became the first Black president, forming government.

The 'Ready to govern' campaign is a masterclass

in strategic communication and transformation. ANC's vision under this campaign had four key messages that were profound: 1) strive for a united South Africa, 2) overcome inequality and injustice in a progressive and principled way, 3) develop a sustainable economy and 4) promote a sense of freedom and security within its borders. Mandela's role in this campaign was pivotal – he wasn't just the face of it, he embodied the message.

For anyone looking to drive change, be it in politics, business or any organisational setting, this campaign offers great insights. It teaches us that the right words, chosen carefully and delivered with conviction, can indeed move mountains. This is what we're aiming to achieve in this third part of the UNLOCK Method, expanding followers by spreading awareness.

'Do or Die'

When it comes to using powerful campaign (program) names, there's also another iconic political freedom story that I would be remiss to not mention. It is Mahatma Gandhi's 'Quit India' campaign to free India from the oppressive British rule of the early 1940s.

Gandhi is respectfully known as the father of India. Mahatma is the title given to this inspiring personality who led the masses with his optimism, courage, principles, patience and persistence.

Gandhi played a pivotal role in securing freedom for India. As a strong advocate of 'Satya' (truth) and 'Ahimsa' (non-violence), Gandhi showed the power of love and non-violence to contest injustice and oppression.

To keep this brief, the British had been occupying India since 1600, at first in the interest of trade, and later for political reasons. By World War II, sentiment in India was starting to shift and the local Indian population was calling for an end to British rule. An effort by the British to secure Indian support for World War II in return for self-governance was rejected by India's Congress, at which point Gandhi realised that the situation had reached a critical point. He knew the locals would join his movement against the British at a national level. He went full throttle and started the 'Quit India' movement, making his landmark 'do or die' speech on 8 August 1942.

This is what Gandhi said in that speech:

> *Here is a mantra, a short one that I give you. You may imprint it on your hearts and let every breath of yours give expression to it. The mantra is: 'do or die'. We shall either free India or die in the attempt; we shall not live to see the perpetuation of our slavery.*

Many of the leaders of this movement were jailed, and thousands of average individuals took to the streets in protest against the Brits. The determination of the Indian people pushing for independence overwhelmed the British, and after the end of the World War II, the demand for independence could no longer be ignored.

> 'Be the change that you wish to see in the world.' – Ghandi

Five years after the 'Quit India' movement was launched, India achieved independence from British rule on 15 August 1947. Many attribute the power of the 'do or die' mantra to the push for the final uprising. Such is the power naming a campaign.

Gandhi, a barrister qualified from University College London, is most popular for his famous quote, 'Be the change that you wish to see in the world'.

Beyond the Benchmark

Let's switch from politics back into the corporate and academic world. If you're looking for a good book to read on managing change, *Switch: How to Change Things When Change Is Hard* by brothers Chip Heath and Dan Heath is a great read. This *New York Times*–

best-selling book provides compelling examples that demonstrate the profound impact of naming change programs and initiatives.

One of the most notable case studies, and my favourite, is from British Petroleum (BP). In the late 1990s, Ian Vann, the new head of global exploration at BP, faced a critical challenge. BP was experiencing escalating costs, and Vann noticed that BP was operating with just a 20% (one in five) accuracy rate when exploring for new oil sources. However, they were the industry benchmark!

Determined to change things around, and not satisfied with being best in class at 20%, Vann declared a bold new strategy named 'No dry holes'. This radical directive, which was initially met with resistance and shock from the explorers, had a profound impact on the mindset.

By 2000, BP had improved their drilling accuracy to a staggering 66% – a dramatic improvement from their previous 20% accuracy. This turnaround not only boosted BP's efficiency and profitability, but also showcased the power of succinctly naming strategic initiatives.

This is the reason why many global companies have named their supply chain excellence programs – to improve ownership and acceptance. Here are a few examples:

- Bega: BEX (Bega Excellence)
- BHP: BOS (BHP Operating System)
- Canon: CPS (Canon Production System)
- Danone: DaMaWay (Danone Manufacturing Way)
- Diageo: ManEx (Manufacturing Excellence)
- Ferrero: FOX (Ferrero Operational eXcellence)
- Ford: FPS (Ford Production System)
- Glaxo: GPS (GSK Production System)
- Kellogg: KWS (Kellogg Work System)
- McDonalds: MOS (McDonalds Operating System)
- Nestle: NCE (Nestle Continuous Excellence)
- P&G: IWS (Integrated Work System)
- Toyota: TPS (Toyota Production System)

Looking at these names, we can see that – clearly – supply chain individuals aren't a creative bunch. I was in the room with the global team when we created KWS, inspired by P&G's IWS program. However, in a world where social media platforms are called 'X' (previously Twitter) and celebrities name their children 'Apple', these names are not that bad.

Naming something creates a tangible identity to anything, including human beings. Think about change

> Changing our behaviours and maintaining lasting results can only happen through embracing the identity of the new person you want to be.

initiatives in personal development. We know that changing our behaviours and maintaining lasting results can only happen through embracing the identity of the new person you want to be. For example, if we want to be a healthy person, we know that we have to change the narrative in our head as to who we are, who we've been and how we currently see ourselves – our current identity – to what a healthy person would do and look like, and embrace that new identity. I slightly digress here as this is not a personal development book, but I feel compelled to share this because I have found it to be key to my success in my journey as an entrepreneur for the last nine years.

So, it is the same with our corporate change initiatives. We are trying to name and brand our major change journey so that it will help improve the chances of acceptance and adoption by teams and individuals. It will help create an identity for the journey. That's what Mark did.

You need to keep your ears to the ground. This is when you will be approached by the 'unusual ones', the 'quiet ones'. They may comment when you're in the canteen making a coffee and having a casual chat. Something has changed in these individuals. Something has resonated with them. You

> Name major change journeys so that it will help to improve the chances of acceptance and adoption by teams and individuals.

need to strike while the iron is hot. Give them something to work with. Leverage their ego – in a good way.

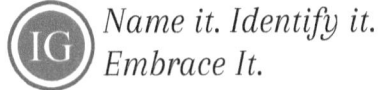
Name it. Identify it. Embrace It.

CHAPTER 11

Leverage Their Ego

'If you can dream it, you can do it.'
– Walt Disney

Sanjeewa migrated to Australia in early 2015 with zero work experience in the commercial world. However, that wasn't Sanjeewa's biggest challenge – his proficiency in the English language was extremely low. He knew that these were major roadblocks, but Sanjeewa was used to the curveballs that life throws.

'It wasn't easy', said Sanjeewa. 'Growing up in a developing country like Sri Lanka, I lived in a rural setting, away from the capital and the big cities. We didn't get the privileges of the big cities. Having access to English teachers in school was one of those.' The second son of a family of four boys, he remembers growing up in a very small house, but one that was overflowing with love, courage and motivation. 'I saw my father, a carpenter, working with manual tools to earn a hard living to care for the family. Seeing how they [his parents] struggled to provide a better future for us, I wanted to advance in life and look after them.'

It's that courage that got him to stand in line to join the Sri Lankan Air Force on his 18th birthday, during the last stage of the horrific 30-year terrorist war in Sri Lanka. His parents opposed it, but when they realised that he was determined, they backed down. To his surprise, his father said, 'Son, make sure you do it well, and remember, do not come home halfway through it if you realise it is too tough. I'll drag you back. I didn't raise any of my boys to be quitters in life!' This provided a lesson in life that he has lived by ever since.

It is the same mindset that helped Sanjeewa secure his first role in a manufacturing company in Perth, Western Australia, a couple of months after migrating. It was a large company with multiple sites, so Sanjeewa was encouraged to do even better to grow within. Although he was learning different processes and machines, his poor language skills felt like his biggest hurdle.

> 'Learn a new skill everyday – that's what I wanted to do, and still do', Sanjeewa said.

However, through turns of other life events, Sanjeewa and his wife found themselves in Sydney – in the big city! With his positive attitude in life and at work, it wasn't too hard for Sanjeewa to secure a transfer to one of the Sydney sites at the same company. There was one set back though: he would have to go back to being a Level 1 operator at the bigger Sydney site due to the way that site recognised the competencies required to attain different levels. The highest is Level 5 – the supervisory level.

By working diligently and always putting his hand up for training and opportunities, Sanjeewa learnt many skills and competencies in a short period of time.

He even got his forklift licence on his own through a private training organisation. 'Learn a new skill every day – that's what I wanted to do, and still do', Sanjeewa said.

It is that mindset that saw him putting his hand up for a manual handling course to become the safety champion of the shift. 'My supervisors weren't that confident, but I somehow convinced them.' During the week-long training, Sanjeewa discovered that he had to deliver a 15-minute presentation back at the site. He felt his heart beating faster as he wondered how he was going to do it. Somehow, he delivered his first presentation to the site leadership team. 'I can't remember how I did it, it is bit of a blur, but I remember the feeling when I finished. My fingertips were shaking and felt like I'd had 10 coffees. Must be the adrenaline', said Sanjeewa, laughing it off.

Sanjeewa was now getting noticed, particularly by his team leader who took him under his wing. Sanjeewa loved it and absorbed all the coaching he could get. Many of Sanjeewa's work colleagues, mainly the big blokey alpha males on shift, would tease him as he was still a Level 1 operator despite years of learning. They said that the leaders and the company were taking advantage of his eagerness to learn by skilling him up for their advantage and not for Sanjeewa's benefit. That didn't deter Sanjeewa, who'd been through tougher situations during his childhood and in the military as a young adult.

By the time I met Sanjeewa in 2022, he was working as the second-in-charge (2IC) for the day shift under the team leader who'd coached him. 'Do you know what the funny thing is, Ishan?' asked Sanjeewa during one of our chats. 'When I was appointed 2IC, I went from Level 1 straight to Level 5. I don't think there's anyone who has achieved that', he said with his chest slightly puffed. He further explained how he's now coaching those colleagues who teased him and who are still where they were in terms of the competency grading system. I could only think of the 'Tortoise and the Hare' parable that we heard as children. A real-life story of how slow and steady can win the race, I thought.

When I met Sanjeewa, the company he was working for had signed up to go through an operational excellence transformation and I was privileged to walk alongside the site leadership team, guiding, coaching and mentoring. The site had identified two major improvement initiatives to work on initially. Sanjeewa was selected as a team member for one of those projects. During our interactions, I saw Sanjeewa as someone the team relied on, someone who always got things done and a friendly person who cracked jokes to energise team.

It wasn't until much later that I learnt that Sanjeewa had to put in a lot of effort to overcome his 'I'm not good enough' mindset. It is amazing how repeated thought patterns shape our subconscious mind to the point that we actually start believing them.

> It is amazing how repeated thought patterns shape our subconscious mind to the point that we actually start believing them.

It is a bit like well-formed forest walking trails that get created by hundreds of repeated steps through what was once a thick forest. The first person to walk through the forest, much like our first thought in a new way of thinking, will require significant effort, hacking through the uncharted territory. Once the trail is formed, you'll be walking along that in shorts without much thought or effort. The same is true about the path in your neural network that you have now created through repeated firing of the same synapses.

What's important is that we can all rewire and reprogram new beliefs or habits, but it requires conscious re-programming of the subconscious. Given the complexity of this topic and what I want to get out of this chapter, I will keep this at surface level. There is

> What's important is that we can all rewire and reprogram new beliefs or habits, but it requires conscious re-programming of the subconscious.

a short cut that we can all use when reprograming our mindset – particularly when you want to feel confident and that voice in your head is speaking through a megaphone telling you that you're not good enough.

If you're keen to explore this a bit more, I recommend watching two TED talks. The first one is by Harvard professor Amy Cuddy, titled 'Your Body Language May Shape Who You Are'. During her undergraduate years, Cuddy was involved in a serious car accident and suffered a severe head injury. While the doctors said that she would struggle to fully regain her mental capacity and finish her undergraduate degree, Cuddy proved them wrong. Her research today is on nonverbal behaviour and judgements that affect people. The *New York Times*–best-selling author shares that you can fake it until you make it, in a positive sense, to reprogram your subconscious.

The other TED talk is by Benjamin Zander, the conductor and musical director of the Boston

Philharmonic Orchestra and the Boston Philharmonic Youth Orchestra, titled 'Life Lessons from Beethoven's Symphony No. 9'. Through his unusual style of presenting mixed with his piano performances on stage, he takes his audiences on a journey of learning through classical music. In this TED talk, he shares his thoughts on the difference between 'positive thinking' and 'possibility', with stories from one of the greatest composers of all time – Beethoven – as well as one of his student's greatest achievements.

Sanjeewa proved both Cuddy's and Zander's theories. The first round of projects was immensely successful. Sanjeewa, along with the project lead and the rest of the team, presented to multiple leadership teams.

During the second round of projects, his team leader wasn't available at a critical time as his wife had just given birth to their son. The team leader was meant to provide an update to the state director, the national director and the operational excellence director. With just a weekend's notice, Sanjeewa stepped up and presented on behalf of his team leader. He'd come a long way since his first presentation after the manual handling training!

Sanjeewa's progression in his career, through sheer determination and hard work, is definitely admirable, but it is not too hard to find such individuals in most organisations. Yes, we hear about their passion and what's in it for them, and this is true. In Sanjeewa's case, the need to look after his parents and support his brothers are all 'bigger than self' objectives. It was during a casual chat over a coffee, that he shared what he thought was an insignificant event, which helped me to connect the dots.

I asked him what it meant for him to be involved in the improvement programs. (I wasn't privy to his entire back story at this point.) Sanjeewa mentioned that when he catches up with friends, most of whom are working for equally great companies, they inevitably start talking about work. Many of his friends talk about amazing projects that they are working on. 'I didn't even know what a project was at the time, and I would simply make stuff up to keep up with the conversation', Sanjeewa said in a sheepish way. 'Now, I simply talk about the projects I'm leading, the savings generated – it is part of my normal conversation.'

Right then and there, Sanjeewa demonstrated the theory of the 'hierarchy of needs' developed by the American psychologist Abraham Maslow in the mid-1940s.

Maslow argued that all human beings have needs relating to five key domains: 1) physiological, 2) safety and security, 3) love and belonging, 4) esteem and 5) self-actualisation. He stated that individuals must satisfy the lower-level needs first before they can satisfy the higher-level needs. Also, that the higher we go in the hierarchy, the harder it is to satisfy the needs.

> Maslow argued that all human beings have needs relating to five key domains: 1) physiological, 2) safety and security, 3) love and belonging, 4) esteem and 5) self-actualisation.

Sanjeewa had moved to Australia with his wife and found a place to live, which meets the physiological needs of the first level: water, food, shelter etc. Tick. With his health in good shape, successful career now shaping up, the second level, safety and security, needs are met. Tick. With his loving wife and parents plus a caring team leader, the third level needs are met. Tick. Now comes the fourth level, the esteem needs – the need to be a contributing individual. Sanjeewa hadn't ticked this off yet; it was his next hurdle in life. And the driving factor was his self-worth – a powerful driver.

Sir David R. Hawkins was a renowned psychiatrist, physician and researcher, and an author in the field of consciousness. In one of his books titled *Power vs. Force,* Hawkins introduces the 'map of consciousness', a scale quantifying the levels of human consciousness. It ranges from low (guilt, shame) to high (love, enlightenment), suggesting a person's emotional state affects their life experiences and interactions. The important thing here is that the lowest of the low emotional states of consciousness, as per Dr Hawkins, is the state of shame. Which is what Sanjeewa was feeling when he was with his friends.

> If you can leverage the right person's ego in a positive and morally correct way, then you can find people who will take charge and come up through the ranks to follow you.

So, if you can leverage the right person's ego in a positive and morally correct way, then you can find people who will take charge and come up through the ranks to follow you. This is exactly the path that Sanjeewa took. In fact, some individuals would even risk their lives for self-esteem, which was proven just over a century ago.

Test of Endurance

In the early 20th century, Sir Ernest Shackleton, an Anglo-Irish explorer, embarked on a dangerous Antarctic journey, marking a tale of survival against all odds. His first Antarctic adventure was in 1901, but it was in 1907 that Shackleton led his own expedition, the Nimrod expedition, coming frustratingly close to the South Pole and earning a knighthood upon his return.

On 1 August 1914, Shackleton set sail on his most ambitious project – crossing Antarctica from the Weddell Sea to the Ross Sea. Commanding the *Endurance*, Shackleton and 27 men set sail from London, coincidentally the same day Germany declared war on Russia (World War I). Tragedy struck in January 1915 when the *Endurance* became trapped in the Weddell Sea ice. After nine agonising months, the crushing ice claimed the ship. Stranded, Shackleton's party camped on the shifting ice, their situation growing increasingly desperate.

In a daring move, Shackleton and five men embarked on an 800-mile journey across treacherous seas, leaving the rest on Elephant Island. After a demanding 15-day journey, they reached South Georgia, only to land on its uninhabited side. Shackleton, navigator Frank Worsley and Tom Crean embarked on a gruelling 36-hour trek across the island's uncharted terrain, eventually reaching a whaling station in the town of Stromness.

Meanwhile, those left on Elephant Island faced their own battle for survival. It wasn't until 30 August 1916, after multiple failed rescue attempts, that Shackleton, successfully rescued his crew. Every member survived, a testament to Shackleton's extraordinary leadership.

Shackleton died in 1922, aged 47, while on another expedition in South Georgia. His death marked the end of an era of heroic Antarctic exploration. Shackleton's story is one of courage, resilience and leadership. While he may not have achieved his goal of crossing Antarctica, his legacy endures in the extraordinary tale of survival, human spirit and exploration.

Now, imagine that you've time travelled to 1914, and you see a newspaper advert that reads, 'Men wanted for hazardous journey, small wages, bitter cold, long months of complete darkness, constant danger, safe return doubtful, honour and recognition in case of success'. Would you put your hand up?

Although the origins of this advert are a bit unclear and unverified, it has been quoted in many places and often quoted in relation to Shackleton's *Endurance* expedition. If we entertain the idea that it was printed, then what was Shackleton trying to leverage? The individual's ego, self-esteem, self-worth, confidence, sense of achievement and respect from others. The fourth-level needs that Maslow would identify several decades later.

Springbok's Success

If we time travel back, but land at the other end of the 20th century, 1995 to be precise, we'd be in the middle of the rugby World Cup hosted in post-apartheid South Africa.

This story has been brought to life by the movie *Invictus*, directed by Clint Eastwood. It portrays how Nelson Mandela, (played by Morgan Freeman) demonstrates the remarkable power of leveraging people's egos in a positive manner to foster outstanding commitment and results.

Mandela recognised that the nation needed a unifying force, and he found it in the South African rugby team, the Springboks. Instead of viewing them as symbols of the old 'White' regime, he saw an opportunity to use their success as a source of pride and

> **Mandela recognised that the nation needed a unifying force, and he found it in the South African rugby team, the Springboks.**

> Mandela effectively harnessed the players' egos and desire for success.

unity for the entire country. By reaching out to the team's captain, François Pienaar (played by Matt Damon), and instilling in him a sense of purpose and national pride, Mandela effectively harnessed the players' egos and desire for success.

This strategic move ignited exceptional commitment and determination within the team. The players, once motivated by personal pride and the desire to make their nation proud, achieved astonishing results playing against the mighty New Zealand team and winning the 1995 Rugby World Cup.

In *Invictus*, Mandela's leadership demonstrates that by leveraging individuals' egos in a positive way and providing opportunities for them to feel proud of their contributions, organisations can inspire outstanding commitment and success.

The stories in this chapter serve as powerful examples of how visionary leadership and a well-placed sense of pride can bring about transformative changes in individuals and teams to strive to deliver outstanding results.

You can now step off the time travel capsule in present time.

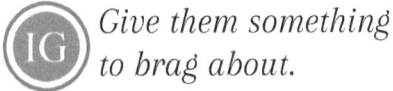

Give them something to brag about.

CHAPTER 12

A Rising Tide Lifts All Boats

'Surround yourself with only people who are going to lift you higher.'

– Oprah Winfrey

In April 2008, Tim Morgan, the site leader for Players Biscuits Company (PBC), a subsidiary of Arnott's Biscuits at the time, had a tough challenge. The parent company had decided to shut down PBC for strategic reasons, and he had eight months to plan and execute the shutdown while keeping the business running and the employees safe and engaged. I joined Tim's leadership team a couple of months later as the operations manager and, therefore, had a front-row seat to witness how he went about executing this tough project with empathy.

> Lead the site celebrating when possible, improving where relevant, but above all, caring for everyone all the time.

Tim demonstrated how to lead the site celebrating when possible, improving where relevant, but above all, caring for everyone all the time, despite the tough decision that had been made by head office. To this date, nearly everyone who worked on that site talks about the wonderful experience of working as a team at PBC in Miranda – a southern industrial suburb of Sydney. What was so special and what did Tim do so differently?

PBC became part of Arnott's Biscuits when Arnott's

acquired SnackBrands, which owned PBC. When I joined Tim's team, he welcomed me the only way he knew how – by making me feel valued, wanted and cared for. He does this tirelessly and effortlessly with every group and every individual. Tim was known for his humble and caring leadership style within the Arnott's Group.

Here's one example of this – in my early days at the new site, I was in his office having a one-on-one chat when his mobile phone rang. The screen was facing down, so he didn't know who was calling, and he simply muted it without even checking who was calling and without breaking eye contact with me. A few seconds later, his office phone rang and there was a strong possibility that it could be the same person. He let it ring out. I asked, 'Do you want to take it? It could be from head office?' After all, the site was heading to shutdown in a few months and there were plenty of serious

> Tim had the same effect on the entire site, and he did it authentically, willingly and caringly. This is how he led that site, keeping its sprits and morale high until the very last day.

decisions to be made and signed off. Tim's reply was, 'This is our time. If it's important, they'll call back. I'll tell them that I was with one of my team members.' I felt six inches taller at the time, but felt bad later on when I found out that it was the chief supply officer, Tim's boss. Tim had the same effect on the entire site, and he did it authentically, willingly and caringly. This is how he led that site, keeping its sprits and morale high until the very last day.

Geoff Player founded PBC back in 1974 with multiple confectionary lines with various capabilities. It was able to manufacture most of the products in the sweets aisle, and a significant part in the biscuit aisle in Australian supermarkets. With its capabilities, the site manufactured chocolate and chocolate products, wafer biscuits, cookies, marshmallow and sweet biscuits. The iconic Arnott's wagon-wheel biscuit, bringing back fond childhood memories to many Australian adults, was also manufactured at the PBC site.

The overall site capabilities hadn't changed significantly over time and Arnott's certainly invested in the site to bring it up to its own standards. However, this is not what made PBS special. There was a special ingredient, a special vibe: the people who worked there. What was so different about this site that it won 'site of the year' award from the Arnott's Group more than once?

The site had about 125 full-time employees and perhaps another 30 casuals working across three shifts from Monday to Friday. Most of the people had been there since the beginning. Two things were clear to me as I got to know them: first, most of them would not work again and would take an early retirement; and second, there was a level of comradery that I hadn't seen anywhere else before.

> The upper limit of meaningful social connections one person could hold is 150. This is now known as the Dunbar number.

On a side note, there's also a scientific basis as to why this site (with about 125 to 155 employees) had a higher level of cohesiveness: the Dunbar number. In the 1990s, British anthropologist Robin Dunbar found a correlation between primate brain size and the average social group size. He suggested that the upper limit of meaningful social connections one person could hold was 150. This is now known as the Dunbar number.

Apart from the coincidental employee numbers that just happened to be convenient to foster a great culture, there were a number of specific things that Tim was relentless on:

- **Individual connections**

    Tim would religiously go around to all shifts every week, making sure that he talked to all operators – joking around, asking how they are and so on. It was mainly small talk, but it provided an opportunity for a pulse check of the vibe on the floor. Of course, having the site leader do that meant the rest of the site leadership team did it as well – especially me, as the operations manager. It's amazing what you pick up on these rounds and conversations: who's feeling down, who's overwhelmed, who's celebrated a milestone birthday or an anniversary etc. All very important data points to keep the team together and feeling supported.

- **Town hall communication**

    Keeping communication channels open with regular town halls was critically important to keep the rumour mill turning slow. It was also important for the employees to hear everything that concerned them, including how the company was performing. Despite the impending shut down in a few months' time, they really wanted to do well, and they cared for the company. The employees loved hearing about their success from fellow employees. So, often we'd get the key individuals to speak and present during these sessions.

- **Creative monthly fun themes**

    Having fun was right up there on Tim's priority list, and we had a theme each month. For example, in August 2008 during the Beijing Olympics, the site held a month-long mini-Olympics; another month was dedicated to karaoke singing, with a karaoke machine in the canteen. The main purpose was to provide a fun energetic environment until the last day.

- **Food to connect**

    Who doesn't love food? For every reason we could find that we thought was good enough to celebrate, we organised a site barbecue. And these crews went to town on some of these barbecues – it wasn't just sausages, bacon and eggs on toast. I remember Asian stir fry dishes, Middle Eastern breads and salads, slow-cooked meat etc, all done on site.

- **Slogan**

    Slogans tend to drive us, as we found out in Chapter 10. The site had a massive banner in the canteen that read 'Finishing with Pride', which was something that the team came up with. That reminded them every day how they wanted to be remembered.

Tim's ethos around leadership is to create an infectiously happy environment so that it lifts even those who are feeling down. A rising tide certainly lifts all boats.

Everyone who wanted to stay with the Arnott's Group was given priority for existing vacancies within the company to continue their employment. Others who took their payout were extremely happy as, true to his style, Tim ensured that those individuals were looked after.

> Create an infectiously happy environment so that it lifts even those who are feeling down.

At the same time, there were other big companies who were forced to shut down their sites for various reasons. I remember seeing their logos across media channels, with unions and employees protesting and creating havoc. PBC and Arnott's didn't have any of it, simply because of one man, the right person with the right leadership skills who led it with heart. Tim Morgan continued his employment at Arnott's, eventually becoming the chief supply officer for the Arnott's Group.

Exemplary Customer Service

Nearly a decade before the shutdown of PBC, in 1999 to be exact, an online shoe retailing company called Zappos was started in the US by entrepreneurial friends Nick Swinmurn, Tony Hsieh and Alfred Lin. Zappos is considered one of the best companies to study employee engagement and outstanding performance. It's not surprising, then, that leaders from companies known for service and quality, such as Southwest Airlines and Toyota, make regular visits to learn from Zappos. The man who created all this is Tony Hsieh, who led Zappos as the CEO from 1999 until 2020, when he sadly passed away aged 46.

Tony Hsieh graduated from Harvard in 1995 – a year that significantly changed everything in the world as we know it today. In January 1995, Jerry Yang, a Stanford graduate, registered the domain Yahoo.com, and the search engine was born. In March 1995, Craig Newmark started an email distribution list to friends, which later evolved into Craigslist, and online classified advertising was born. In April 1995, Match.com was launched, revolutionising the way people meet and date virtually, and online dating was born. In July 1995, Jeff Bezos founded Amazon.com from his garage in Seattle, initially a small online bookstore, and online retailing was born.

The following year, in 1996, Hsieh and his Harvard friend Sanjay Madan co-founded LinkExchange, an internet advertising network. LinkExchange quickly gained traction and, in November 1998, Microsoft purchased LinkExchange for an impressive $265 million.

In 1999, Hsieh met Nick Swinmurn, who introduced him to the idea of selling shoes online, and Zappos was born. The vision was clear from the beginning: create a company that's not just about selling shoes but about delivering the best customer service and experience.

Since then, it has become an exemplar of an employee-centric environment, which was spearheaded by Hsieh, as CEO, until his death in 2020. Hsieh's philosophy was to encourage employees to be the same person at home and in the office, fostering authenticity and comfort. This approach is deeply rooted in Zappos' culture and is reflected in their 10 Core Values:

1. Deliver WOW through service.
2. Embrace and drive change.
3. Create fun and a little weirdness.
4. Be adventurous, creative, and open-minded.
5. Pursue growth and learning.
6. Build open and honest relationships with communication.

7. Build a positive team and family spirit.
8. Do more with less.
9. Be passionate and determined.
10. Be humble.

One of the key aspects of Zappos' work environment is allowing employees to express their individuality. The casual dress code and personalised workspaces, where employees can display personal items and vibrant decorations, illustrates this. This freedom of expression is not just superficial, it extends to empowering employees to explore their passions and express creativity. For instance, an employee with a knack for improv comedy evolved from a mailroom position to a senior trainer, demonstrating the company's commitment to employee growth and passion.

> Freedom of expression is not just superficial, it extends to empowering employees to explore their passions and express creativity.

Zappos also places a strong emphasis on continuous learning. Their training team, Pipeline, offers various classes with creative names like 'Pimp my PowerPoint' and 'Tighten your Team', showing a blend of fun and professionalism. This dedication to growth and learning is a part of Zappos' larger mission to inspire employees and expose them to diverse thinking.

Central to Zappos' philosophy is the empowerment of employees, especially in customer service decisions. This autonomy allows employees, irrespective of their position, to make decisions that enhance customer satisfaction, embodying their core value of 'Deliver WOW through service'. For example, call-centre employees have the freedom to refund a customer's money, upgrade shipping or send surprise packages to customers, fostering a sense of ownership and responsibility among the staff. And there are many stories of how employees have gone above and beyond to WOW their customers.

The company's focus on employee happiness is a critical factor in its success. Zappos provides various benefits, including an on-site life coach to help employees achieve personal and professional goals. This approach has led to transformative experiences for many employees, further aligning their personal values with those of the company.

Zappos' unique approach to employee engagement can be quantified. For instance, when their call centre moved from the Bay Area to Las Vegas, an astonishing 80% of its California employees relocated, demonstrating deep commitment and loyalty. In

2008, when the average turnover at call centres was 150%, Zappos' turnover was just 39%, which included promotions. This low turnover rate is attributed to the company's culture that cultivates passion, purpose and humanity.

The *Zappos Culture Book*, an insightful publication containing employees' unscripted comments about the company's culture, is a testament to the impact of their work environment. It highlights the importance of being oneself and the removal of fear in the workplace, which are crucial for creativity and engagement.

By prioritising the customer experience, Zappos has established itself as a leader in online retail. Zappos' journey showcases the profound impact of a workplace culture that values employee empowerment, continuous learning, individual expression and, above all, happiness. This culture has not only led to a highly engaged workforce, but has also created a loyal customer base, driving the company's success in the competitive online retail space.

In 2009, Amazon acquired Zappos for a staggering US$1.2 billion. Even after the acquisition, Zappos retained its unique culture, becoming a model for companies wishing to enhance customer service and employee engagement.

If you're looking for a great book on this topic, *The Happiness Advantage: The Seven Principles of Positive Psychology That Fuel Success and Performance at Work* by Shawn Achor articulates the profound impact of a positive and happy culture, coupled with clear and open communication, on achieving outstanding results.

Achor, drawing on extensive research and real-world examples, introduces the concept of the 'happiness advantage', where a positive mindset primes the brain for improved performance. He explores how cultivating a workplace culture entrenched in positivity and happiness can lead to higher levels of engagement, creativity and productivity among employees.

> Create an infectiously happy and energetic environment to elevate everyone's performance to the next level.

Achor's insights show that when people feel valued, connected and empowered to communicate openly, they're more likely to collaborate effectively, solve problems and innovate, ultimately leading to outstanding results.

The Happiness Advantage is a compelling reminder that happiness isn't a by-product of success, it's a catalyst for it. By cultivating a positive and open culture, organisations can harness the happiness advantage to achieve remarkable outcomes.

Create an infectiously happy and energetic environment to elevate everyone's performance to the next level. Remember, a rising tide lifts all boats.

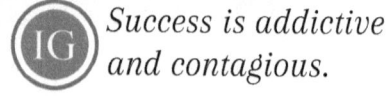
Success is addictive and contagious.

Conclusion

*'You can't talk yourself
out of a problem that you
behaved yourself into.'*

– Stephen Covey

When I was about six years old, I went on a family holiday by train in Sir Lanka. It was a long journey, about five to six hours, heading into the hills district in the middle of the country, casually referred to as the 'up country'. You may have heard of the main city in this district, Kandy, which was a capital city of the country way before the British landed.

Up country has a beautiful landscape, with lush green tea plantations on the slopes of the mountains. The road winds around the mountain to slowly make its way to the top, passing beautiful waterfalls along the way. The train, of course, cuts through the mountain tunnels in the most straightforward line as practically as possible. Even within this small island of Sri Lanka, which is a tad smaller than Tasmania and about three-quarters of the size of Ireland, there are so many climatic zones, from the tropical beaches to rainforests to cold mountain ranges, allowing holiday makers to choose from a variety of destinations.

On this trip, I noticed that every time the train stopped there was a lot of movement and jerking when it started moving again. This was particularly pronounced as we approached the hilly areas. I asked my father why the train jerked so much at the start. He explained that as the train stops at an incline, all the carriages and the couplings are under tension. And the poor old diesel engine doesn't have enough power to pull the entire train uphill from a standstill. I have to admit, as I wrote that last line, I felt like that was a line from a *Thomas the Tank Engine* series. Poor Thomas was struggling under the load, but he wasn't ready to give up puffing, 'I think I can, I think I can', as he let off a puff of steam. I digress again.

With the entire train under tension, the engine doesn't have enough torque to get going. This is not quite the case with the new diesel engines, but back in the day they got around this issue by a technique called 'taking the slack'. My father explained, 'The engine releases the brakes momentarily to release the tension and the carriage moves downhill slightly, except the last one that holds the entire train. This is the backward movement. Then, as the engine starts pulling forward, it only needs to pull the first carriage as it is the first coupling to come under tension.'

My father demonstrated it with his hands. He created a chain link by using the thumbs and the index fingers of his two hands and creating two interlocking circles. He then showed me what happens when the tension is released and tensioned again as the engine starts to pull forward. When the first carriage starts moving, it creates tension in the coupling between the first and the second carriage, and so on and so forth. Therefore, the load on the engine is only increasing one carriage at a time.

These are the train jerks I felt, going backwards and then moving forward along with the bangs, booms and thuds! It is amazing that the same diesel engine that struggles to get going can gain great speeds once it builds up momentum. All from the same engine!

This is exactly how I want you to gain momentum in your business too. You will not have enough capacity and bandwidth to run multiple projects and initiatives at the start. So, pick what's comfortable for you. With most sites, I start with two initiatives, three if it is a bigger site.

> You will not have enough capacity and bandwidth to run multiple projects and initiatives at the start. So, pick what's comfortable for you.

> Once the teams get the hang of it and you've built the capability in them, you can decide how many initiatives you need to deploy as per your strategic plan.

Once the teams get the hang of it and you've built the capability in them, you can decide how many initiatives you need to deploy as per your strategic plan.

When thinking of this, I could not resist thinking about the Flywheel metaphor that the great Jim Collins talks about in his *New York Times*–best-selling book *Good to Great*. Collins says that it takes a lot of effort to get the first revolution turned. Then it is somewhat easier with the second turn. When you keep turning the handle over and over and over again, going faster and faster in each turn, it gets to a stage where the flywheel can be turned effortlessly, running under its own momentum.

Following Collins' framework, here is the UNLOCK Flywheel.

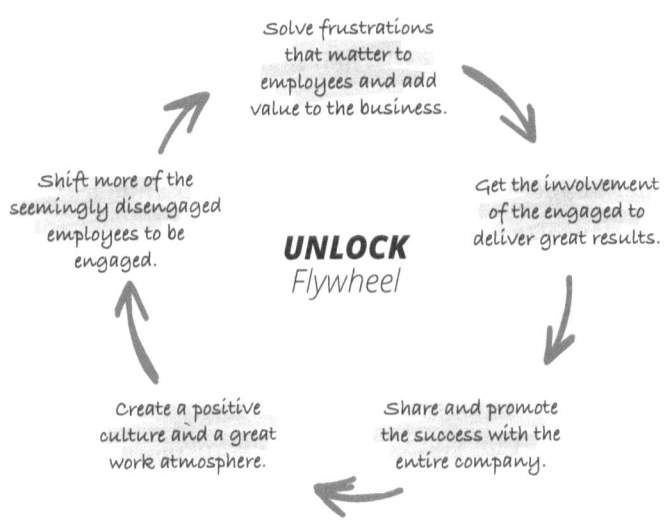

Figure 7: The UNLOCK Flywheel

For the flywheel to be a proper one, it must pass one test. Each specific step of the flywheel has to be an inevitable outcome due to the previous step. Let's see if the UNLOCK Flywheel stands this test.

Firstly, we start by solving frustrations that matter to employees and add value to the business. Now, when we do that, the engaged individuals *almost can't help* but get involved and deliver great results with these initiatives. They do this because they care. They are engaged. Now, we strategically involve a few seemingly disengaged individuals in these initiatives to get them excited by osmosis. When the teams deliver great results, they *almost can't help* but share and promote their great work with their fellow employees in formal and informal settings. When that happens, you *almost can't help* but end up with a positive and a buzzing work culture where success is celebrated regularly. When that happens, you *almost can't help* but shift some of the fence sitters to get interested and be engaged – particularly those who have been part of those projects. And, when you have a growing number of engaged individuals, you *almost can't help* but solve more issues that frustrate the employees and deliver value for the company. And you've tuned one revolution of the flywheel within one business quarter.

> Don't forget that each quarter has a compounding effect as you are generating more and more engaged employees.

Now after the second, third, fourth and fifth revolutions, how many initiatives do you think you will have completed? Don't forget that each quarter has a compounding effect as you are generating more and more engaged employees. Do you not think that after 18 months, you'll have more than enough employees to get the process to a tipping point? At which point, you should be able to continue turning the flywheel relatively easily, and a world-class operation should be within reaching distance. I'll end with the following revision of the fable that I initially shared in the preface.

> *This is a story about four people named*
> *Everybody, Somebody, Anybody and Nobody.*
>
> *There was an important job for the crew.*
> *Everybody jumped in, not waiting for Somebody else to.*
>
> *Nobody stood out and Anybody could pitch in.*
> *Everybody worked together with a grin.*
>
> *Somebody led with a gentle hand.*
> *Everybody brought their hearts of grand.*
>
> *Anybody could've avoided, but Everybody stood tall.*
> *For in this team Nobody was small.*
>
> *All the jobs were done first time right.*
> *Nobody sought for glory and might.*
>
> *Everybody knew that quick-wins shine.*
> *Somebody did it, in this team so fine.*
>
> – Ishan Galapathy

UNLOCK Leadership Assessment

If you're inspired to learn more about yourself – the type of leader you are, and how you could become a leader who can easily unlock true excellence in your organisation – then take the UNLOCK leadership assessment.

Understand the different 'unlocking' leadership styles (e.g., liberator, kindler, warrior, taskmaster) and their benefits and limitations.

Head to:

https://ishangalapathy.com/books/quizzes/ or scan the following QR code.

Actions to UNLOCK Your Team/Organisation

Now you have the inspiration to unlock true excellence in your team and organisation; however, you may be unsure whether to turn left or right, metaphorically speaking. I want to share some practical steps to help bridge the gap. If you run into any hurdles, drop me a note at ishan@ishangalapathy.com. I'll do my best to get back to you.

I update these actions from time to time based on new experiences and insights, which you can find at **https://ishangalapathy.com/books/quizzes/** or by scanning the following QR code.

Before You Begin

Think about the major transformation initiatives that have been launched in your organisation over the last 10 years. How successful have they been? If there are key leads still in the organisation, they could be a great starting point to learn what has worked and what hasn't in the past.

If the transformations in the past haven't been successful, then be mindful that employees have memories like elephants – they remember for a long time. Think about how you would respond to comments such as, 'we've tried this in the past', 'people [leaders] like you come and go but we're still here', 'how are you going to maintain the improvements?' If you meet this kind of resistance, be humble and acknowledge that the organisation could've done better in the past and that we need to learn and move on.

Let's get started then, shall we?

STEP 1: BUILD MOMENTUM

Chapter 1: Value Your Values

- What are the issues that frustrate employees? What do they complain mostly about (other than not enough pay)?

- What are the areas/products that keep you up at night? Which strategic initiatives, if implemented without hassles, would benefit the organisation significantly right now?
- Are there any corporate values or issues that are important to your site (or yourself personally) that you can think of?
- If the above three points were Venn diagrams, what are the initiatives that intersect with at least two circles – best if they intersect all three.

Chapter 2: Believe in Them

- Who are your good soldiers that you can rely on? How tired are they? Can you ask these individuals if they can lead a small project for two to three months. Can you get them out of their current role to completely focus on the initiatives. Who are the employees and promising stars who can step up temporarily and take over the vacant roles? Seconding your leads to initial projects is not essential but hugely beneficial – short-term pain for long-term gain.
- How confident are you with coaching? Can you find the time to coach your disciples? Set up regular catch-ups – I suggest twice a week to begin with.
- Carefully choose who from the seemingly disengaged category you want to include in the project teams.

Chapter 3: What's Your Side Hustle?

- If you need more individuals to step up, ask around (directly or through other department managers) for who'd be capable of stepping up temporarily. Have you thought about asking for expressions of interest? You might be surprised by who knocks on your door.
- During casual conversations, ask people about their hobbies, interests and past experiences. You never know what you might be able to dust off and leverage.

STEP 2: GAIN TRACTION

Chapter 4: It's Not Me; it's You!

- Asking employees 'why we can't get 100% every day' is how I've kicked off every project for the last 25 years. You will need strong facilitation skills to uncover the 'gold nuggets' after the initial not-so-useful reasons.
- Make sure the answers to the above question are all problems and not solutions. We want to know what's getting in their way, their problems, their frustrations. Basically, anything that makes them go home and kick the cat!
- Prioritise top issues by giving everyone three votes for the top three issues they'd like resolved first.

Chapter 5: Give it a Go

- Create a culture where employees feel safe to take risks. You can create safety nets to encourage employees to problem-solve without fear of being reprimanded – a time period they are allowed to troubleshoot on their own before escalating, permission to trial new ideas as long as they don't compromise safety or quality, for example.

- Allocate free time or create small cross-functional groups to discuss issues that frustrate employees and brainstorm new solutions.

Chapter 6: SMART Factories and DUMB Operators

- If you use digital dashboards in huddle meetings, ask attendees to describe the dashboard in their own words and ask them what insights they draw from the information. Ask them which metrics are useful and valuable. Explore what other metrics could be introduced that would be of value to the team.

- If you don't use digital dashboards, create analogue boards with printed metrics in an easy-to-understand visual format. I love getting started this way. I believe in making huddle meetings effective first (analogue) and then efficient (digital). You can download easy-to-print visual templates through the QR provided at the beginning of this section or at **https://ishangalapathy.com/books/quizzes/**.

- When solving problems, show trends using simple Pareto charts and ask people what they think the cause is. Make sure you focus on the causes, not the solutions.

Chapter 7: Start with Who

- When you are about to implement some changes in the workplace, ask two questions:

    1) Whose work is directly impacted by this change? Make sure you speak to these individuals.

    2) Who has the power (officially or unofficially, with a title or without a title) to influence the changes in a positive or negative way? Consult and leverage these individuals.

- Remember: We all love change. We just don't like being changed. So, how are you interacting with the team or individuals to make them feel that they are involved and in control? Don't do it for them. Do it with them.

Chapter 8: Flaws and Fortunes

- Mistakes in the workplaces are often dealt with as performance management. At Toyota, they praise the operator for highlighting a deficiency in the

process that led them to making that error. Fix the process error with the person to eliminate the risk of that error being repeated. At Toyota (Japan), they call this *poke-yoke* (error proofing).
- We all have our strengths and our weaknesses. Do you work hard to improve your weaknesses or double-down on your strengths and outsource the weaknesses?

Chapter 9: Adapting to Triumph

- In order to revise any original tactical planned actions, first you need to know that there has been a deviation from the original 'flight path'. How good is your governance structure and lead indicators to detect these deviations?
- Focus on what's in your sphere of control and influence the next level up. There's not much to be gained by wasting your resources on things that cannot be controlled.

STEP 3: EXPAND FOLLOWERS

Chapter 10: Name it

- Christen projects with names that are meaningful. Bring them alive with logos and slogans.
- Create visuals and place them in high traffic areas, such as workplaces, the canteen, meeting slides

etc. Help people connect their small activities with the bigger picture.

- Don't just make slogans, live them! Find ways to reward individuals and teams that embody the meaning of the slogan.

Chapter 11: Leverage Their Ego

- Ask individuals involved with driving change what it means to them to be involved and implementing these changes. Help those individuals to further leverage those meaningful contributions.

- Find ways to display and promote meaningful messages unearthed from the previous step in places where other employees can see them (canteen, hallways, meeting rooms etc). You could even hire a freelancer to create beautiful posters.

- During casual conversations, ask individuals what they would do if they didn't have to work for the pay (i.e., if money wasn't an issue, what interests would they pursue). See if there are areas that you could support for a win-win outcome; for example, if someone would love to be a travelling YouTuber, then you might have someone you can leverage to cerate promotional videos for your own internal comms.

Chapter 12: A Rising Tide Lifts All Boats

- Do you have quarterly town hall meetings or regular team meetings that bring everyone together? If not, that's your first action. If you already have a forum like this, then think about who speaks at these meetings? Is it mainly you, as the leader, or someone from the site leadership team? Find ways to invite employees to share their success stories. It is easier and more powerful for employees to hear about changes and progress from their peers than a leader on a pedestal.
- Find ways and opportunities to celebrate. Look to infuse positivity into the team.

CONCLUSION

During team meetings, or when celebrating wins as per Chapter 12, don't forget to help individuals connect the dots between their current activities and the end goal – the reason why you are doing what you are doing. Over time, the consistency of this action and seeing progress that includes the employees themselves will be the key to unlocking your team's true excellence.

About the Author

Ishan has a passion for helping business leaders in supply chains (businesses that are either making or moving something) to get more from their businesses than they thought possible.

As an operational excellence strategist renowned for his simplified techniques, Ishan works with businesses to implement the fundamental systems and processes, as well as develop the leadership capabilities, both at site and frontline levels, resulting in unlocked excellence, amplified profitability and improved engagement.

Having worked across seven countries for over two-and-a-half decades with multinationals such as Kellogg's and Arnott's, Ishan has a wealth of knowledge in the field of operational improvement. In his last corporate role at Kellogg's, Ishan was responsible for operational excellence (OpEx) for Asia Pacific. He was also the global lead for continuous improvement and was instrumental in developing Kellogg's global supply chain excellence framework.

Ishan holds a Bachelor of Engineering (Mechatronic) from the University of New South Wales (UNSW), an MBA from Sydney Graduate School of Management (SGSM) and a Six Sigma (black belt) qualification. He has appeared on several media platforms and industry events sharing his thought leadership on OpEx.

He is the author of *Hidden Growth Opportunities,* in which he highlights why many businesses struggle to improve their bottom line while growing the top line, and *ADVANCE: 12 Essential Elements to Supercharge Productivity and Profitability*, which provides a simplified 'paint-by-numbers' operational excellence framework to enable readers to get more from less in an effective and sustainable way.

When he's not working, Ishan is involved in his life passions that are centred on his family. You can find him spending time with his sons while teaching them to drive, cooking up a storm in the kitchen or sipping a cup of coffee with his wife in the garden.

Ishan believes that success is a process, and that latent potential can be turned into profitable growth through an engaged culture. This is his mantra to do more, grow more and be more.

More information at IshanGalapathy.com and you can contact Ishan at ishan@ishangalapathy.com

Acknowledgements

This was not the next book I was planning to publish – that needs a bit more time. In the meantime, in response to some of the needs in the field I was observing, *UNLOCK* emerged. That meant a lot of planning in a short period of time and a team who came together with a lot of flexibility to make this a reality.

First and foremost, I'm most grateful to the individuals who shared their experiences and stories with me, enabling me to draw key insights. I'm also thankful that they have allowed me to share these with the world, allowing many others to learn from these insights and be inspired.

To the business leaders who placed their trust in me to unlock excellence in their teams and organisations. With each new team, I get the opportunity to improve and refine my thinking. This *UNLOCK* framework was born out of these collective experiences.

To my mentors, coaches, supporters and friends, I'm grateful for your inspiration, support and wisdom.

To my book production/publication team: Similar to the saying 'it takes a village to raise a child', it takes an amazing team to bring a book to the world. Without the fabulous editing and feedback by Lu Sexton, this manuscript would be a crappy first draft. Melanie Dankel, I really appreciate your flexibility in the proofread and also, for providing invaluable feedback. Sylvie Blair, for making everything relating to printing and publishing possible and seamless. Celeste Davidson, Karen Klaich and Cris Iconomu for your help with graphics, designing and the website. The advance readers, for your feedback and endorsements to truly refine the content from different perspectives. And finally, Maria Richardson, my chief of staff, for coordinating all these individuals within tight timelines. To all of you, I'm extremely grateful. Thank you.

To my parents, Manel and Siri Galapathy – with more of my hair going grey, I'm realising the importance of the solid foundations of excellence you've laid for my life. Immense gratitude and love.

To my sister, Rukshinie, for continuing to show me the spiritual path to advance and to stay grounded.

To my darling wife and soulmate, Priyanka – nothing is too hard or impossible for you. I'm inspired by the world you're trying to create for humanity and your dedication. Thank you for your love and support for over 28 years and many more to come.

To my beloved sons, Ravin and Hiran – for giving me a big reason to excel in life. Thank you for your love, hugs and the memories we create.

Finally, to the reader – thanks for reading this book and for allowing me to present some ideas to *UNLOCK* excellence and latent capacity in your teams.

References

Introduction

- 'Indicator of Employee Engagement', Gallup23, https://www.gallup.com/394373/indicator-employee-engagement.aspx, accessed December 18, 20.

- 'How to Improve Employee Engagement in the Workplace', Gallup, https://www.gallup.com/workplace/285674/improve-employee-engagement-workplace.aspx, accessed December 18, 2023.

- 'Research Briefings - RP01-38', UK Parliament Commons Library, https://commonslibrary.parliament.uk/research-briefings/rp01-38/, accessed December 18, 2023.

- 'Election Results and Voting Information,' Federal Election Commission, https://www.fec.gov/introduction-campaign-finance/election-results-and-voting-information/, accessed December 18, 2023.

- 'Election Results 2008 - President Votes', The New York Times, https://archive.nytimes.com/www.nytimes.com/elections/2008/results/president/votes.html, accessed December 18, 2023.

- 'President Map - Election Results 2008', The New York Times, https://archive.nytimes.com/www.nytimes.com/elections/2008/results/president/map.html, , accessed December 18, 2023.

- 'BJP's 31% Lowest Vote Share of Any Party to Win Majority', The Times of India, https://timesofindia.

indiatimes.com/news/BJPs-31-lowest-vote-share-of-any-party-to-win-majority/articleshow/35315930.cms, accessed December 18, 2023.

- 'Election Results 2014: India Places Its Faith in Moditva', The Times of India, https://timesofindia.indiatimes.com/news/election-results-2014-india-places-its-faith-in-moditva/articleshow/35224486.cms, accessed December 18, 2023.

- 'Why the World Quit on Quiet Quitting', Gallup, https://www.gallup.com/workplace/507650/why-world-quit-quiet-quitting.aspx.

- 'Globally, Employees are Engaged but Stressed', Gallup, accessed December 18, 2023, https://www.gallup.com/workplace/506798/globally-employees-engaged-stressed.aspx, accessed December 18, 2023.

- Bryan Robinson, '6 Signs That a Quiet Quitter is Among Your Employees and What to Do About It', Forbes, https://www.forbes.com/sites/bryanrobinson/2022/08/19/6-signs-that-a-quiet-quitter-is-among-your-employees-and-what-to-do-about-it/, accessed December 18, 2023.

- Abrashoff, D. Michael. *It's Your Ship: Management Techniques from the Best Damn Ship in the Navy.* New York: Warner Books, 2002.

- Samrat Saha, It's Your Ship: Comprehensive Chapter Wise Summary, Simplified MBA, https://www.simplimba.com/its-your-ship-comprehensive-chapter-wise-summary/, accessed January 21, 2024.

STEP 1: BUILD MOMENTUM

- Vuylsteke, Jena, Joseph Rantz 1914-2007, University of Washington Magazine, https://magazine.washington.edu/joseph-rantz-1914-2007/, accessed January 21, 2024.

- Waxman, Olivia B., The Story Behind The Boys in the Boat, Time, https://time.com/6548861/the-the-boys-in-the-boat-true-story/, accessed January 21, 2024.

- Wilkes, Jonny, The Boys in the Boat: The real history behind George Clooney's underdog sports movie, History Extra, https://www.historyextra.com/period/20th-century/the-boys-in-the-boat-true-story-real-history/, accessed January 21, 2024.

- Embassy of Sri Lanka in Sweden, Horton Plains, https://www.stockholm.embassy.gov.lk/en/sri_lanka/horton-plains/, accessed January 21, 2024.

- Lonely Planet, World's End, https://www.lonelyplanet.com/sri-lanka/the-hill-country/horton-plains-national-park-and-worlds-end/attractions/world-s-end/a/poi-sig/1195264/357476/, accessed January 21, 2024.

Chapter 1: Value Your Values

- 'George Cadbury', Wikipedia, last modified December 24, 2023, https://en.wikipedia.org/wiki/George_Cadbury, accessed December 24, 2023.

- 'Our History', Cadbury Australia, https://www.cadbury.com.au/our-history, accessed December 24, 2023.

- 'George Cadbury', Encyclopaedia Britannica, https://www.britannica.com/biography/George-Cadbury, accessed December 24, 2023.

- 'The Bournville Story', Bournville Village Trust, https://www.bvt.org.uk/wp-content/uploads/2011/03/The-Bournville-Story.pdf, accessed December 24, 2023.

- Phil Preston, *Connecting Profit with Purpose*, Micheal Hanrahan Publishing, 2020.

- Pink, Daniel H., *Drive: The surprising tryth about what motivates us*, Penguin Putnam Inc, 2009.

- Sinek, Simon, *Start with Why: How great leaders inspire everyone to take action*, Portfolio, 2009.

- Sisodia, Raj, Jag Sheth, David B. Wolfe. *Firms of Endearment: How world-class companies profit from passion and purpose,* Pearson, 2014.

- 'Global top25 Supply Chain', Gartner, https://www.gartner.com/en/supply-chain/research/supply-chain-top-25, accessed December 30, 2023.

- Bailey, Adrian Raymond, Bryson, John R., 'A Quaker Experiment in Town Planning: George Cadbury and the Construction of Bournville Model Village', Quaker Studies Vol 11 Issue 1, 2007

Chapter 2: Believe in Them

- QuickRead, Trillion Dollar Coach, https://quickread.com/book-summary/trillion-dollar-coach-360, accessed December 28, 2023.

- Campbell, Bill, 'Trillion Dollar Coach Summary and Review', StoryShots, https://www.getstoryshots.com/books/trillion-dollar-coach-summary/, accessed December 28, 2023.

- Batko, M, Trillion Dollar Coach, Medium, https://medium.com/mbreads/trillion-dollar-coach-4a7e5d25af55, accessed December 28, 2023.

- Hill, Linda, How to manage for collective creativity, TED Talk, https://www.ted.com/talks/linda_hill_how_to_manage_for_collective_creativity?, accessed June 20, 2022.

- Frankel, David, director, *The Devil Wears Prada* [film], Fox 2000 Pictures, 2006.

- Eagle, Alan, Schmidt, Eric, Rosenberg, Jonathan, *Trillion Dollar Coach: The leadership handbook of Silicon Valley's Bill Campbell*, HarperCollins, 2019.

Chapter 3: What's Your Side Hustle?

- May, Brian, Bradley, Simon, *Brian May's Red Special: the story of the home-made guitar that rocked Queen and the world*, Carlton Books, 2020.

- May, Brian, *A Survey of Radial Velocities in the Zodiacal Dust Cloud*, Springer, 2008.

- Lewis, Michael, *Moneyball: The Art of Winning an Unfair Game*. New York: W. W. Norton & Company, 2004.

- Miller, Bennett, director, *Moneyball* [film], Columbia Pictures, 2011.

STEP 2: GAIN TRACTION

- O'Connell, Andrew, 'Lego CEO Jørgen Vig Knudstorp on leading through survival and growth', Harvard Business Review, https://hbr.org/2009/01/lego-ceo-jorgen-vig-knudstorp-on-leading-through-survival-and-growth, accessed January 22, 2024.

- Lutz, Ashley, 'Lego made 3 changes to become the world's most powerful toy company', Business Insider, https://www.businessinsider.com/legos-turnaround-strategy-2015-5, accessed January 22, 2024.

- 'At LEGO, Growth and Culture Are Not Kid Stuff, An Interview with Jørgen Vig Knudstorp', Boston Consulting Group, https://www.bcg.com/publications/2017/people-organization-jorgen-vig-knudstorp-lego-growth-culture-not-kid-stuff, accessed January 22, 2024.

- LEGO, 'The beginning of the LEGO Group', https://www.lego.com/en-my/history/articles/b-the-beginning-of-the-lego-group/, accessed January 22, 2024.

Chapter 4: It's Not Me; it's You!

- Meyers, Nancy, director, *The Intern* [film], Warner Brothers, 2015.

- 'Case Study: Employee innovation at Innocent', Engage for Success, https://engageforsuccess.org/case-studies/case-study-employee-innovation-at-innocent/, accessed December 30, 2023.

- Hickman, Martin, 'Healthy eating trend sees sales of smoothies soar' Independent, https://www.independent.co.uk/life-style/health-and-families/health-news/healthy-eating-trend-sees-sales-of-smoothies-soar-430711.html, accessed December 30, 2023.

- 'Smoothie operators: learning lessons the innocent way', Business & Industry, https://www.businessandindustry.co.uk/employee-wellbeing/smoothie-operators-learning-lessons-the-innocent-way/, accessed December 30, 2023.

- Rachel Sharp, 'Smoothie does it: HR at Innocent Drinks', https://www.hrmagazine.co.uk/content/features/smoothie-does-it-hr-at-innocent-drinks/, accessed December 30, 2023.

- 'Was this an Innocent transaction by Coke?', EXP, https://www.theexpgroup.com/blog/was-this-an-innocent-transaction-by-coke-or-was-it-one-of-5-forces/, accessed December 30, 2023.

Chapter 5: Give it a Go

- Reiner, Rob, director, *A Few Good Men,* Castle Rock Entertainment, 1992.

- Brown, Brené. *Dare to Lead: Brave work. Tough Conversations. Whole Hearts,* New York: Random House, 2018.

- Levy, Steven. *In The Plex: How Google thinks, works, and shapes our lives*, Simon & Schuster, 2021.

- Vise, David A., Malseed, Mark. *The Google Story*, Delta, 2006.

- Schmidt, Eric, Jonathan Rosenberg. *How Google Works*. New York: Grand Central Publishing, 2014.

- Nick Statt, 'Google Co-Founders Larry Page and Sergey Brin Relinquish Control of Alphabet to CEO Sundar Pichai', The Verge, https://www.theverge.com/2019/12/4/20994361/google-alphabet-larry-page-sergey-brin-sundar-pichai-co-founders-ceo-timeline, accessed January 3, 2024.

- 'Larry Page,' Encyclopaedia Britannica, https://www.britannica.com/biography/Larry-Page, accessed January 3, 2024.

- 'Our Story,' Google, https://about.google/intl/ALL_au/our-story/, accessed January 3, 2024.

- Battelle, John, 'The Birth of Google', *Wired*, https://www.wired.com/2005/08/battelle/, accessed January 3, 2024.

- Hartmans, Avery, 'The Life and Career of Larry Page, the Co-Founder of Google and the CEO of Alphabet', Business Insider, https://www.businessinsider.com/larry-page-alphabet-google-life-career-photos-2017-8, accessed January 3, 2024.

Chapter 6: SMART Factories and DUMB Operators

- Shetterly, Margot Lee. *Hidden Figures: The American dream and the untold story of the Black women mathematicians who helped win the space race*. William Morrow, 2016.

- Melfi, Theodore, director, *Hidden Figures* [film], 20th Century Fox, 2016.
- Launius, Roger D. 'NACA to NASA to Now: The frontiers of air and space in the American century', NASA, https://www.nasa.gov/history/history-publications-and-resources/nasa-history-series/naca-to-nasa-to-now/, accessed January 3, 2024.
- Dorothy Vaughan, NASA24, https://www.nasa.gov/people/dorothy-vaughan/, accessed January 3, 2024.
- Mary Jackson, Britannica, https://www.britannica.com/biography/Mary-Jackson-mathematician-and-engineer, accessed January 3, 2024.
- Dorothy Vaughan, History of Scientific Women, https://scientificwomen.net/women/vaughan-dorothy-103, accessed January 3, 2024.
- Katherine Johnson, History of Scientific Women, https://www.scientificwomen.net/women/johnson-katherine-100, accessed January 3, 2024.
- Mary Jackson, History of Scientific Women, https://www.scientificwomen.net/women/jackson-mary-104, accessed January 3, 2024.
- Hutchman, Lorna, 'Dorothy Vaughan: Nasa's overlooked star', Science Museum, https://blog.sciencemuseum.org.uk/nasas-overlooked-star/, accessed January 3, 2024.
- IBM 7090 Data Processing System, IT History Society, https://www.ithistory.org/db/hardware/ibm/ibm-7090-data-processing-system l, accessed January 3, 2024.

- Harris, Robin, 'Hidden Figures and the IBM 7090 computer', ZDNet, https://www.zdnet.com/article/hidden-figures-and-the-ibm-7090-computer/, accessed January 3, 2024.

- Jacobs, Caleb, 'VW Is Putting Buttons Back in Cars Because People Complained Enough', The Drive, https://www.thedrive.com/news/vw-is-putting-buttons-back-in-cars-because-people-complained-enough?_hsmi=287209010, accessed January 3, 2024.

- Hidden Figures, SparkNotes, https://www.sparknotes.com/lit/hidden-figures/, accessed January 3, 2024.

- Hidden Figures, https://www.hiddenfigures.com/, accessed January 3, 2024.

- Van Sant, Gus, director, *Good Will Hunting* [film], Miramax Films, 1997

Chapter 7: Start with Who

- Frost, John, 'How internal rivalry at Disney animation impacted The Lion King and Pocahontas', The Disney Blog, https://thedisneyblog.com/2015/06/25/how-internal-rivalry-at-disney-animation-impacted-the-lion-king-and-pocahontas/, accessed December 26 2023.

- 'Jeffrey Katzenberg', Britannica, https://www.britannica.com/biography/Jeffrey-Katzenberg, accessed December 26, 2023.

- 'The Life of Jeffrey Katzenberg: Co-founder of DreamWorks', PeoPlaid, https://peoplaid.com/2020/12/21/jeffrey-katzenberg/, accessed December 26, 2023.

- Golembewski, Vanessa, 'The Secret Rivalry Between Pocahontas & The Lion King', Refinery29, https://www.refinery29.com/en-us/2015/06/89430/pocohantas-disney-anniversary-animation-team-rivalry, accessed 26-Dec-23.

- Persall, Steve, 'Katzenberg: the prince of animation', Tampa Bay Times https://www.tampabay.com/archive/1998/12/08/katzenberg-the-prince-of-animation/, accessed December 26, 2023,.

- 'More Scar', Deja View, https://andreasdeja.blogspot.com/2011_09_21_archive.html, accessed December 26, 2023.

- Sinek, Simon. Start with Why: How great leaders inspire everyone to take action, Penguin, 2009

- Sinek, Simon, How great leaders inspire [video], TED talk, https://www.ted.com/talks/simon_sinek_how_great_leaders_inspire_action/, accessed February 10 2011.

Chapter 8: Flaws and Fortunes

- Belludi, Nagesh, 'Creativity—It Takes a Village: A Case Study of the 3M Post-it Note', Right Attitudes: Ideas for Impact, https://www.rightattitudes.com/2021/04/15/creativity-case-study-post-it-note/, accessed December 24, 2023.

- History Timeline: Post-it Notes, Post-it, https://www.post-it.com/3M/en_US/post-it/contact-us/about-us/, accessed December 24, 2023.

- Art Fry & Spencer Silver Post-it® Notes, Lemelson-MIT, https://lemelson.mit.edu/resources/art-fry-spencer-silver, accessed January 5, 2024.

- Spencer Silver, National Inventors Hall of Fame24, https://www.invent.org/inductees/spencer-silver, accessed January 5, 20.

- Arthur Fry, National Inventors Hall of Fame, https://www.invent.org/inductees/ Arthur-l-fry, accessed January 5, 2024.

- The Invention of the Post-it® Note, National Inventors Hall of Fame, https://www.invent.org/blog/trends-stem/who-invented-post-it-notes, accessed January 5, 2024.

- Post-It, History Timeline: Post-it® Notes, https://www.post-it.com/3M/en_US/post-it/contact-us/about-us/, accessed 5-Jan-2024

- Spencer Silver, co-inventor of 3M Post-it® Notes, dies at 80, 3M News Centre, https://news.3m.com/Spencer-Silver,-co-inventor-of-3M-Post-it-R-Notes,-dies-at-80, accessed January 5, 2024.

- 3MHistory, 3M, https://www.3m.com/3M/en_US/company-us/about-3m/history/, accessed January 19, 2024.

Chapter 9: Adapting to Triumph

- 'Reed Hastings', Forbes, https://www.forbes.com/profile/reed-hastings/?sh=3f4d311d2782, accessed January 23, 2024.

- Kollewe, Julia, 'Fangs' Breakneck Rise: Facebook, Amazon, Netflix, Google, The Guardian, https://www.theguardian.com/business/2017/apr/29/fangs-breakneck-rise-facebook-amazon-netflix-google, accessed January 23, 2024.

- 'Reed Hastings', Encyclopaedia Britannica, https://www.britannica.com/biography/Reed-Hastings, accessed January 23, 2024.

- 'About Netflix', Netflix4, https://about.netflix.com/en, accessed January 23, 202.

- 'Netflix Market Cap', CompaniesMarketCap.com, https://companiesmarketcap.com/netflix/marketcap/, accessed January 23, 2024.

- 'CEO Reed Hastings on How Netflix Beat Blockbuster', Marketplace, https://www.marketplace.org/2020/09/08/ceo-reed-hastings-on-how-netflix-beat-blockbuster/, accessed January 23, 2024.

- Saul, Derek, 'Netflix Earnings: Subscribers Swell to Record 247 Million as Stock Soars,' Forbes, https://www.forbes.com/sites/dereksaul/2023/10/18/netflix-earnings-subscribers-swell-to-record-247-million-as-stock-soars/?sh=57553d6b64df, accessed January 23, 2024.

- 'Netflix Subscribers', Demand Sage, https://www.demandsage.com/netflix-subscribers/, accessed January 23, 2024.

- 'Marc Randolph', https://marcrandolph.com/, accessed January 23, 2024.

- de Crespigny, Richard. QF32: Life lessons from the cockpit of QF32, Macmillan Australia, 2012.
- Zoom interview with Richard de Crespigny, December 11, 2020
- Howard, Ron, director, *Apollo 13* [film], Universal Pictures, 1995.

STEP 3: EXPAND FOLLOWERS

- Gladwell, Malcolm, *The Tipping Point: How little things can make a big difference*, New York, Little, Brown and Company, 2000.
- Rogers, Everett M., Diffusion of Innovations. New York, Free Press, 2003.
- 'Broken Windows Theory,' Encyclopaedia Britannica, https://www.britannica.com/topic/broken-windows-theory, accessed January 23, 2024.
- Saul McLeod, 'Broken Windows Theory', Simply Psychology, https://www.simplypsychology.org/broken-windows-theory.html, accessed January 23, 2024.
- Davies, Samuel Thomas, 'The Broken Windows Theory and Your Environment', https://www.samuelthomasdavies.com/broken-windows-theory/, accessed January 23, 2024.
- Siegel, Harry, 'Broken windows policing is ineffective and unjust,' New York Daily News, https://www.nydailynews.com/2022/03/31/broken-windows-policing-ineffective-unjust/, accessed January 23, 2024

- Goodwin, Michael, 'How NYC used then tore up broken windows policing', New York Post, https://nypost.com/2020/08/15/how-nyc-used-then-tore-up-broken-windows-policing-goodwin/, Accessed January 23, 2024

- Laughland, Oliver, 'Inside William Bratton's NYPD: 'Broken Windows' Policing', The Guardian, https://www.theguardian.com/us-news/2015/jun/08/inside-william-bratton-nypd-broken-windows, accessed January 23, 2024.

- Moore, Geoffrey A, Crossing the Chasm: Marketing and selling high-tech products to mainstream customers, New York, HarperBusiness,1991.

Chapter 10: Name it

- Grant, Tracy, Nelson Mandela, Britannica4, https://www.britannica.com/biography/Nelson-Mandela, accessed January 11, 202.

- The South African general elections: 1994, South African History Online, https://www.sahistory.org.za/article/south-african-general-elections-1994, accessed January 11, 2024.

- Remembering Gandhi: Top 10 quotes by the Mahatma, Times of India, https://timesofindia.indiatimes.com/blogs/the-photo-blog/remembering-gandhi-top-10-quotes-by-the-mahatma/, accessed January 11, 2024.

- Quit India Movement Day: When Mahatma Gandhi coined famous slogan 'do or die', Zee Business24, https://www.zeebiz.com/india/news-quit-india-

- movement-day-when-mahatma-gandhi-coined-famous-slogan-do-or-die-193199, accessed January 11, 20.
- Bi India Bureau, Business Insider, https://www.businessinsider.in/india/article/mahatma-gandhi-famous-quotes-for-whatsapp-and-facebook-status/articleshow/78408172.cms, accessed January 11, 2024.
- Yadav, Pooja, 'What Was 'Do or Die' Speech of Mahatma Gandhi and How it Shook Roots Of British Rule In India', India Times, https://www.indiatimes.com/explainers/news/what-was-do-or-die-speech-of-mahatma-gandhi-and-how-it-shook-roots-of-british-rule-in-india-577336.html, accessed January 11, 2024.
- Heath, Chip, Heath, Dan, *Switch: How to change things when change is hard,* Crown Publishing Group, 2010.
- KaiNexus, Danielle Yoon, Examples of Companies Using Continuous Improvement to Gain a Competitive Edge, https://blog.kainexus.com/continuous-improvement-companies, accessed January 11, 2024.
- '7 companies that forever changed the face of process excellence', PEX, https://www.processexcellencenetwork.com/innovation/articles/7-companies-that-forever-changed-the-face-of-proce, accessed January 11, 2024.
- Henriques, Cinthia, '7 APAC companies that used Kaizen to achieve operational excellence', PEX, https://www.processexcellencenetwork.com/business-transformation/articles/7-apac-companies-that-used-kaizen-to-achieve-operational-excellence, accessed Janaury 11, 2024.

Chapter 11: Leverage Their Ego

- Cuddy, Amy, 'Your body language may shape who you are', TED Talks, https://www.ted.com/talks/amy_cuddy_your_body_language_may_shape_who_you_are?, accessed January 14, 2024.

- Zander, Benjamin, 'Life lessons from Beethoven's Symphony No. 9', TED Talks, https://www.ted.com/talks/benjamin_zander_life_lessons_from_beethoven_s_symphony_no_9?, accessed January 14, 2024.

- Horn, Joshua, 'Shackleton's Ad – Men Wanted for Hazardous Journey', Discerning History, https://discerninghistory.com/2013/05/shackletons-ad-men-wanted-for-hazerdous-journey, accessed January 14, 2024.

- Shackleton's Voyage of Endurance, Nova Online, https://www.pbs.org/wgbh/nova/shackleton/1914/timeline.html, accessed January 14, 2024.

- Mulvaney, Kieran, 'The Stunning Survival Story of Ernest Shackleton and His Endurance Crew', History, https://www.history.com/news/shackleton-endurance-survival, accessed January 14, 2024.

- Potier, Beth, 'Shackleton in Business School', The Harvard Gazette, https://news.harvard.edu/gazette/story/2004/01/shackleton-in-business-school/, accessed December 24, 2023.

- Sir Ernest Shackleton, Royal Museums Greenwich, https://www.rmg.co.uk/stories/topics/sir-ernest-shackleton, accessed January 14, 2024.

- Hawkins, David R, *Power vs. Force: The Hidden Determinants of Human Behavior,* Veritas Publishing, 1995.
- Eastwood, Clint, director, *Invictus* [film], Warner Brothers Pictures, 2009.

Chapter 12: A Rising Tide Lifts All Boats

- Achor, Shawn, *The Happiness Advantage: The seven principles that fuel success and performance at work*, New York: Currency, 2010.
- Au-Yeung, Angel, Jeans, David, *Wonder Boy: Tony Hsieh, Zappos, and the myth of happiness in Silicon Valley,* New York: Henry Holt and Company, 2023.
- Dunbar's number: Why we can only maintain 150 relationships, BBC Future, https://www.bbc.com/future/article/20191001-dunbars-number-why-we-can-only-maintain-150-relationships, accessed January 15, 2004.
- Mitchell, Sur, 'Biscuitmaker to Go Public to Join the Big Players', Financial Review, https://www.afr.com/politics/biscuitmaker-to-go-public-to-join-the-big-players-19911120-k4nsf, accessed January 15, 2004
- Tjan, Anthony K., 'Four Lessons on Culture and Customer Service from Zappos CEO, Tony Hsieh', Harvard Business Review, https://hbr.org/2010/07/four-lessons-on-culture-and-cu, accessed January 15 2004
- Frei, Frances, Morriss, Anne, Uncommon Service: How to win by putting customers at the core of your

business, Harvard Business Review, https://www.hbs.
edu/faculty/Pages/item.aspx?num=41980, accessed
January 15, 2004.

- Dr. Vivek Pandey, The Zappos Model: How Delivering
  Happiness Transforms Business and Leadership,
  LinkedIn, https://www.linkedin.com/pulse/zappos-
  model-how-delivering-happiness-transforms-business-
  pandey/, accessed January 15, 2004.

- Pascual, Mig, 'Zappos: 5 out-of-the-box ideas for
  keeping employees engaged, US NEWS, https://
  money.usnews.com/money/blogs/outside-voices-
  careers/2012/10/30/zappos-5-out-of-the-box-ideas-
  for-keeping-employees-engaged, accessed January 15,
  2004.

- 'Before Zappos: The inside story behind Tony Hsieh's
  first millions', FAST COMPANY, https://www.
  fastcompany.com/90873958/tony-hsieh-linkexchange,
  accessed January 15, 2004.

- Siampani, Anna, 'CEO Spotlight: The story of Tony
  Hsieh, an innovative entrepreneur', CEOWORLD
  MAGAZINE, https://ceoworld.biz/2020/11/18/
  ceo-spotlight-the-story-of-tony-hsieh-an-innovative-
  entrepreneur, accessed January 15, 2004.

Conclusion

- Collins, Jim, *Good to Great: Why some companies make the leap... and others don't,* Harper Business, 2001.

www.ingramcontent.com/pod-product-compliance
Lightning Source LLC
Chambersburg PA
CBHW022041290426
44109CB00014B/935